Nathan Lorick abandons mere conjecture and focuses on reality! *Dying to Grow* is the work of a gifted writer who has hammered out the principles of effective evangelism on the anvil of his own life. In an era that calls for a renewed sense of urgency to reach others for Christ, this book will lay soul winning at the front door of your heart.

**Tom Elliff**
**President, International Mission Board**
**Southern Baptist Convention**

Church leaders are desperate for help – looking for clarity and vision. Reading this book will make you feel like you are talking with someone who understands this struggle. Nathan challenges you to see how a Kingdom focus can bring fresh life to your personal walk and church.

**Al Gilbert**
**Vice President, Evangelism**
**North American Mission Board, Southern Baptist Convention**

I love what my friend Nathan Lorick is saying: "This book is a simple and concise challenge to abandon the desire for church growth and to embrace the heart of growing Christ's Kingdom." Such a shift demonstrates both a biblical reality and a present need. Such a shift will free pastors from the bondage of performance and yet lead to effective ministry. This helpful book will encourage, inspire, and convict!"

**Alvin L. Reid, Ph.D.**
**Professor of Evangelism and Student Ministry/Bailey Smith**
**Chair of Evangelism**
**Southeastern Baptist Theological Seminary**

If your church is "Dying to Grow", then you need to take this book seriously. Dr. Nathan Lorick writes from the heart of a Pastor, because that is where he cut his spiritual teeth in ministry. Trust me, the lessons in this book were not contrived in an ivory tower by an out-of-touch academician, rather they were learned (sometimes painfully!) in the day-to-day trenches of real ministry! I strongly encourage you to read carefully, then apply plentifully!

**David A. Wheeler, Ph.D.**
**Professor of Evangelism, NAMB Field Missionary, &**
**Director of Center For Ministry Training**
**Liberty University**

We are living in a time when the gospel has become the greatest story never told. A time when we are giving our first-class loyalties to third-class causes. A time when we fill our lives with good things to the exclusion of the best things. A time when evangelism is no longer the obsession of our lives. In a time like this, it is refreshing to hear the voice of one who exists for evangelism as fire exists for burning. Thank God for Nathan Lorick and this book *Dying to Grow*. I wholeheartedly and enthusiastically recommend that you read this work.

**Charles Roesel**
**Pastor Emeritus, First Baptist Church of Leesburg, FL**

Nathan Lorick confirms from scripture that pursuing those who need Christ is more than Church Growth; it is Kingdom Advancement. He illustrates the biblical text through life experiences that engage and challenge. He points to the need to move beyond numbers to the practical application of planning and the power of God. It is well worth the read.

**Jim Richards**
**Executive Director, Southern Baptists of Texas Convention**

*Dying to Grow* is an honest evaluation of where we are in many churches. We have lost our desperation for God and in turn lost our passion for sharing the Gospel. We may fill the pews, but the presence of the one who can change lives, the culture, and the world is all but absent. Dr. Lorick has given us a tremendous tool that is both passionate in its appeal and practical in its approach.

Any Pastor or church leader would benefit from reading and applying the truths found in this book. May our hearts be stirred so our lives will mirror biblical Christianity. May it be said of us, "for we cannot but speak of the things we have seen and heard."

**Bill Britt**
**President, Compel Outreach International**

Nathan Lorick has written a book that is an important read for pastors and church leaders. *Dying to Grow* addresses the reasons our churches have plateaued and are declining – something everyone should be concerned about. Lorick draws from his pastoring experiences and his passion for evangelism to bring a great perspective to the spiritual battle we face. This book is both prophetic and practical. It is clear and concise. I found myself evaluating our own church's evangelistic strategy through the lens of *Dying to Grow*, and you should do the same. The appendix is a great resource for planning and strategy. It's well worth your time.

**John Meador**
**Senior Pastor, First Baptist Church of Euless, TX**

I, like many pastors, want my church to grow. In *Dying to Grow*, Nathan Lorick calls us back to the one thing and the only thing that can really grow the church, the gospel of Jesus Christ. Nathan passionately challenges pastors and church leaders to go back to making the gospel essential in everything we do and thus making evangelism the key component once again in our ministries and in our lives.

**Robert Welch**
**Senior Pastor, Rock Hill Baptist Church of Brownsboro, TX**

Laypersons, Pastors, and Ministers in every area of Church life should read the book by my friend Dr. Nathan Lorick, *Dying to Grow*. This young Minister of the Gospel has learned and put into practice principles of truth that many of us are still struggling with in the senior years of our lives. This book is a must read! It will bring you to your knees in humility, refocus your life and Church on what really matters, and lead you to faithfully commit to that which is most important to our Heavenly Father. Your life will be changed by its message and you will rest in what it truly means to be God's servant for Jesus' sake.

**Don Cass**
**Retired Director of Evangelism**
**The Southern Baptists of Texas Convention**

Having observed modern ministry leadership and practices, Dr. Nathan Lorick, one of this generation's notable evangelism leaders, correctly concludes: "In the pursuit of growing, we are actually dying because we are forsaking the Great Commission." A former pastor, now evangelism director of the Southern Baptists of Texas Convention, Dr. Lorick weaves personal life experiences with the Scriptures in such a way that anyone, whether serving the pastorate or sitting in the pew, can plainly understand current ministry leadership problems and the biblical answers to solve them.

As an evangelism professor, I especially appreciate two distinctives of *Dying to Grow*. First, Dr. Lorick presents modern evangelism approaches like mercy ministries and media-based ministries without neglecting time-tested methods like door-to-door evangelism and street preaching. Also, I'm deeply grateful that throughout the book he not only addresses a "burden for the lost," an almost-forgotten phrase among believers today, but also he exhorts his readers to adopt a burden for the lost.

If you are satisfied with ministry reflecting secular business models more than sacred biblical principles, *Dying to Grow* will cause you to rethink your position, if not convince you otherwise. If you've all but given up hope that anyone in this generation believes that ministry leadership in the current era can incorporate new and helpful approaches while retaining effective traditional ones, this book is one of the reasons you've kept believing.

**Matt Queen, Ph.D.**
**Assistant Professor of Evangelism**
**Associate Dean for Doctoral Programs**
**Roy Fish School of Evangelism and Missions**
**Southwestern Baptist Theological Seminary**

Nathan hits a home run with this powerful and compelling must-read. Pastors, use this as a field manual to unleash your church's true redemptive and evangelistic potential.

**Paul Mints**
**Lead Pastor, The Community at Lake Ridge of Arlington, TX**
**South Central Regional Director for Growing Healthy Churches**

Nathan Lorick has penned this book in such a way that you will read it and be spurred into action. *Dying to Grow* clearly communicates the need to reclaim the priority of Kingdom growth through intentional evangelism in our churches. If your desire is to see God use your church to transform your city, this book is a must. I encourage you to not only read it, but allow it to be a practical tool as you seek to fulfill the Great Commission.

**Nathan Lino**
**Senior Pastor, Northeast Houston Baptist Church**

Through autobiographical confession and biblical admonition, Nathan Lorick, in his book *Dying to Grow*, reveals the subtle danger of getting caught up in the "success syndrome" of growing a church even when one begins with the best of intentions. The author debunks major myths in ministry that contribute to this all-too-common phenomenon among pastors. Utilizing numerous examples from Scripture with practical principles for the contemporary church, Nathan demonstrates how the pastor can recapture the proper motivation for ministry and evangelism resulting in true Kingdom Growth. He also provides very helpful ways that pastors can rekindle the fire of evangelism in their churches. The descriptive models of evangelism and the excellent ideas for evangelism in the local church contained in the two appendices are worth the price of the book! Every pastor and church leader who is serious about impacting his community with the Gospel needs to get this book, read it, repent, and then re-implement the Great Commission as the purpose and focus of his church for the glory of God and the expansion of His Kingdom here on earth.

**Preston L. Nix, Ph.D.**
**Professor of Evangelism and Evangelistic Preaching**
**Occupying the Roland Q. Leavell Chair of Evangelism**
**Director, Leavell Center for Evangelism and Church Health**
**Chairman, Pastoral Ministries Division**
**New Orleans Baptist Theological Seminary**

# Dying
## to Grow

# Dying to Grow

## Reclaiming the Heart for Evangelism in the Church

**Nathan Lorick**

*Foreword by* **Ed Stetzer**

 ANEKO Press

www.lifesentencepublishing.com

Dying to Grow – Dr. Nathan Lorick

Copyright © 2013

Scripture quotations taken from the New American Standard Bible®, Copyright © 1960, 1962, 1963, 1968, 1971, 1972, 1973, 1975, 1977, 1995 by The Lockman Foundation. Used by permission. (www.Lockman.org)

PRINTED IN THE UNITED STATES OF AMERICA

First edition published 2013

LIFE SENTENCE Publishing books are available at discounted prices for ministries and other outreach. Find out more by contacting info@lifesentencepublishing.com

ANEKO Press, LIFE SENTENCE Publishing, and its logos are trademarks of

LIFE SENTENCE Publishing, LLC
P.O. BOX 652
Abbotsford, WI 54405

Paperback ISBN: 978-1-62245-107-4

Ebook ISBN: 978-1-62245-108-1

10  9  8  7  6  5  4  3  2  1

This book is available from www.lifesentencepublishing.com, www.amazon.com, Barnes & Noble, and your local bookstore

*Cover Design: Amber Burger*

*Editor: Sheila Wilkinson*

# Dedication

———— ⚓ ————

*This book is dedicated to the love of my life, Jenna Lorick. You are the greatest wife, mother, and ministry partner I could ever ask for. This book is only possible because of your selfless love and support for this vision that God placed on my heart. I am eternally grateful that God allowed us to walk this journey of life together.*

# Contents

Dedication ........................................................................ xiii

Foreword, by Ed Stetzer ................................................. xvii

Acknowledgements ........................................................ xix

Introduction ................................................................... xxi

Ch. 1: A Realistic Diagnosis ............................................ 1

Ch. 2: An Unimpressed God ............................................ 9

Ch. 3: Redeeming the Time ............................................ 13

Ch. 4: A Fatal Attraction ............................................... 19

Ch. 5: Dying to Grow .................................................... 27

Ch. 6: Overcoming the Critic ........................................ 35

Ch. 7: A Conversation with God .................................... 43

Ch. 8: The Rifle Factor .................................................. 49

Ch. 9: The Compelling Gospel ....................................... 57

Ch. 10: Reclaiming the Lost Burden .............................. 65

Ch. 11: Motivating and Mobilizing ............................... 73

Ch. 12: Developing the Strategy .................................... 83

Ch. 13: Keys to Implementing Your Strategy ................. 95

Ch. 14: The Faith Test .................................................. 103

Ch. 15: Kingdom Growth .............................................. 109

Ch. 16: Conclusion ....................................................... 117

Appx. 1: Evangelism Models in the Modern Church ..... 119

Appx. 2: Ideas for Evangelism in Your Church ............. 129

About the Author ......................................................... 143

Endnotes ...................................................................... 145

Bibliography ................................................................ 147

# Foreword

There is not a problem with pastors and leaders being concerned with church growth. The issues arise when church growth is defined merely in terms of numerical growth for one local congregation.

Many Christians, reflecting the values of their culture rather than the values of Scripture, are obsessed with being big for its own sake. Cultural standards are pulled into the grid for measuring church success. But is size really the best measurement for church health?

It is my contention that faithfulness and fruitfulness are much more biblical measuring sticks for church health than strictly examining the number of people who attend on a given Sunday morning.

In Dying to Grow, Nathan Lorick confesses his own struggles with seeking big numbers for his church and the advancement of his own kingdom over the making of disciples and the growth of God's Kingdom. In relaying parts of his own story, he calls on church leaders to sacrifice their personal ambitions for the sake of the Kingdom.

While Nathan and I agree that every church leader and member should desire and work toward seeing more people in pews, that should flow from their passion for the making of disciples, the health of their church, and the growth of God's Kingdom as a whole.

Dying to Grow encourages churches to renew their passion for evangelism. LifeWay Research found that fewer and fewer unchurched individuals are visiting churches, necessitating Christians living out a missional, incarnational faith on a daily basis.

Not only does this book provide the theological and biblical underpinning for valuing Kingdom growth and emphasizing evangelism, Dying to Grow provides practical models for personal and church evangelism.

My prayer is that many will apply the principles from this book and find their churches are no longer dying to growing numerically, but rather are growing spiritually to live.

**Ed Stetzer**
President, LifeWay Research
www.edstetzer.com

# Acknowledgements

I want to personally thank:

The team at Life Sentence Publishing. You have been a real joy to work with on this project. I pray God's favor upon your future.

Jayson Larson and Jerry Pierce. You men were such a blessing to me on this journey. I could not have done this without you.

My ministry assistant Sheryl McFadden. Your ministry is a blessing and greatly appreciated. You are making your life count for the Kingdom.

The staff of the SBTC. It is a joy to work alongside of you as we seek to reach Texas and the world with the gospel.

The churches that I have had the honor of pastoring. Your patience, compassion, and love equipped me to write this book.

My four children who sacrificed "daddy time" so that I could focus on what God was calling me to write. I love you and am so thankful for you.

# Introduction

I hate to admit it now.

It's all so subtle; it happens so naturally. Some of it was even driven by good intentions. I was living my life so that I would be considered "successful" in ministry – or, as I say in a later chapter, I was pursuing the ministerial version of the American dream. I wanted plaques and accolades, I desired power and position, I hoped to be the next big thing. I admit it … I was pursuing my own kingdom over His.

And I was a pastor!

I worked tirelessly and went to great lengths to see my church grow. There was nothing I wouldn't do or at least try, to see the numbers rise. I was consumed with church growth, even to the point of neglecting my own spiritual growth.

There I was, a young up-and-comer, yet I was miserable. I had seen God do amazing things. I had experienced some great moments as a pastor, but at the end of the day all I cared about was if my church was growing. I simply became addicted to the concept of church growth and lost my vision for kingdom growth.

This book is a simple and concise challenge to abandon the desire for church growth and to embrace the heart of growing Christ's kingdom. We know through the Scriptures that when the King and His kingdom are the focus, the church will grow. Many pastors and church leaders have gone astray from the very thing that caused the church to explode with growth – evangelism. They have chased misguided dreams of ministerial success and in the process have lost the very purpose for which churches exist: to fulfill the Great Commission. In exchange for drawing a crowd of church hoppers and curiosity seekers, too many churches have failed to preach a transforming gospel message of faith, repentance, and hope beyond this cursed creation.

We have good news – the best news ever – and it's not a mere self-improvement message. It's so much better than that.

I implore you as you read this book to recapture the zeal for what God wants to do in your church through a renewed strategy and passion for evangelism. God desires to orchestrate providential moments in your community. As you pray and obey, God will do more than you can ask or imagine.

# CHAPTER 1

# A Realistic Diagnosis:
## Living with an Unknown Disease

———————— ⚓ ————————

*You are the light of the world. A city set on a hill cannot be hidden.* – Matthew 5:14

I remember it as if it were yesterday.

I sat with my dad on the tailgate of my truck in a hospital parking lot, staring off at the star-filled sky at 3:00 a.m. wondering what the future would hold. Never expected it, never desired it. It was a conversation no one wants to have. Ever.

Earlier that day, my stepmom Maria went in for a routine checkup. She was experiencing some minor discomfort near her abdomen, not anything to be overly concerned about. In fact, from the outside she was the portrait of good health. The doctors figured her problems stemmed from nothing more than a grouchy gallbladder – which is easily treatable with a simple surgery that would have her on her way in a couple of days. At least that's what we thought!

Upon examining her and running tests that included everything from blood to ultrasounds, the unimaginable happened: Maria had developed what the oncologists call stage IIIC ovarian cancer, a type of cancer involving one or both ovaries that had spread to the lymph nodes or to tumors larger than 2 cm that had attached to the inner abdomen. It was the most devastating news our family had ever received. In the blink of an eye, our happy and hopeful expectations turned into uncertainty, and our lives were turned upside down.

Maria was a trooper. She fought a long and hard battle with this wicked disease. She trusted in the Lord while at the same time submitting to His plan. On February 4, 2010, she entered into His eternal presence. You see, on the outside everything looked great. No one would have ever guessed that anything was wrong. However, on the inside, this deadly cancer was waging war with her body.

So many churches today find themselves in the condition that Maria did. Everything seems stable and secure, yet because of an exodus from the biblical model of evangelism, the church is crumbling internally. The church is harboring a disease that is killing it but is unaware of the fact. I am not necessarily talking about attendance or giving. I am speaking of the reality that the church is dying in its enthusiasm and burden. It may look like a growing church and appear healthy, but the reality is the church is slumping on a foundation made of sand, and its walls are ready to tumble to the ground.

On the other hand, the church that we see in the book of Acts is a thriving church. We know according to Acts 2:47 that the Lord was adding to their number day by day those who were being saved. This church was on fire after its experience with the gospel. There was an explosion of people coming to faith in Christ after Peter's sermon, and this awakening set the course, propelling the early church to turn the world upside down.

Out of this movement, missions and organized discipleship were launched, and the world saw the power of the gospel. It was a movement spreading at a rate that churches today could only hope for.

But the reason the church was growing so rapidly wasn't some new strategy put forth by the apostles. It wasn't a program designed in the dimly lit upper room. It wasn't even some model quickly packaged and manufactured after Pentecost. It was much simpler and much more spiritual than these. The church grew so rapidly because of the power of the gospel! That's it. There is no fancy way of saying it. The church grew because Jesus had just given His life as the penalty for our sins. The gospel was the answer, the method, and the model.

Churches today have incorporated so many models and methods and programs that our dependence upon the execution of those things often overshadows our dependence on God to show up and do something supernatural. We have bought into the lie of the enemy that we must have something for everyone in order to grow. Unfortunately, we forsake the gospel in the process of trying to appease everyone, and in this process, we end up dying in our pursuit of growing.

> **We forsake the gospel in the process of trying to appease everyone, and in this process, we end up dying in our pursuit of growing.**

Churches today need to find their way back to the gospel by ignoring the newest self-help church growth books and following the example of the fastest growing and most effective church that history has ever seen – the church in Acts. We must make the tough decision to forsake anything that pulls our attention and pursuit away from the gospel. What we really need is a realistic diagnosis of where we are.

Statistics tell us that each year 3,500 to 4,000 churches in America close their doors for the final time .[1] That is about seventy-five churches each week. This should be alarming to believers today who invest their lives into a local body of Christ. This should be excruciating to ministers who selflessly give themselves daily for the church's advancement. This should be humiliating to the Christian church as a whole, as we have seen a shift in the priority of the church in our lives.

We must wake up and take note. We must see where we are and determine where it is God wants us to go! I believe we see a great picture of this in Mark 10. The story is of a blind beggar named Bartimaeus. He was both physically and financially impaired. Bartimaeus stayed on his street corner day after day, begging for enough money to buy his next meal. On the outside, it looked as if he had no future and no hope. It seemed that his life would never amount to anything more than his current state of being blind and poor. However, this would soon change.

One day on his dusty street corner, he began to hear a rumble. I'm sure he felt the vibration on the ground as a large group of people proceeded through town together. In no time, Bartimaeus heard that Jesus from Nazareth was walking through town. This was the Jesus who had already healed the lame, walked on water, fed five thousand, and even caused another blind man to see. Bartimaeus had to go through this self-diagnosis that we are talking about. He had to walk through a process in his mind and heart before Jesus left the town.

In looking at this story we can understand that Bartimaeus had to go through a three-stage process that ultimately led to him living life in a more fulfilling way than he ever had imagined. This is a great pattern for us and our churches to go through today as well. We will examine these three stages over the next few chapters.

## STAGE 1: REALITY CHECK

In those brief moments, Bartimaeus had to have a reality check. He had to realize where he was in order to know where he wanted to go. He had to have a difficult discussion with himself, acknowledging his lowly state. I can imagine Bartimaeus reminding himself that he could stay on the same corner every day, continuing to beg for his next meal. I can imagine him thinking through the possibilities his life could have if he could only meet Jesus. But first he had to get real about where he was on that day.

It is really no different for our churches. We must realize that perhaps we are not where God wants us to be right now. We must get to the place where we look past the lights and curtains and realistically see our condition. Our future could depend on our present dose of reality.

This happened in a church that I pastored. Full of incredible people, they loved me and my family and followed my leadership. In fact, they even met in a tent outside for six weeks in December and January while we were remodeling our sanctuary. These are the types of people you would want to pastor.

In my first couple of years, the church exploded in growth. Things couldn't have gone better. I was on top of the world in many people's minds. Yet when I laid my head on my pillow at night, I was unfulfilled. I wondered every day how someone in my position could feel that way. I struggled to understand why I didn't feel like we were doing what God wanted us to do.

Then the day came. The same kind of day that Bartimaeus had. A day of honest evaluation about where we were and where I knew God wanted us to be. We were spending our time planning to attract people, when we should have been out ministering to people. We were investing in programs and methods, when we should have been utilizing our resources to meet needs and share the gospel. I spent most of my time speaking about church growth, when my conversations and sermons should have been about kingdom growth.

> **I resolved in my heart that it would be far greater to be what God wanted us to be than what we wanted to be.**

This view of reality for me was painful. I didn't want to change the way I did ministry. I didn't want to lead my church away from the very things that were causing us to grow so quickly. However, I resolved in my heart that it would be far greater to be what God wanted us to be than what we wanted to be.

This was the heart of Bartimaeus. He knew that he had problems. He knew that there was absolutely nothing he could do about it. He knew that he was all he was ever going to be apart from an encounter with the Master. This is where many churches are today. You are what you are always going to be unless you experience a new vision from God. I challenge you to take a good, honest evaluation and get a realistic understanding of where you are and where you need to be. Once I did this in our church, we began to see where God was leading us.

Church leaders, take an honest, unbiased look at where you are. Look at what you are filling your time with as a church. Look at where you are investing your money. Listen to what you are talking about most among your people. Run the tests and see if you are mirroring the church in Acts. This church was built on the gospel. That was its strategy. That was its model. That was its method. That is why we need to embrace the reality of where we are and look to the future with anticipation.

# CHAPTER 2

# An Unimpressed God:

## Desperation Is the Key to God's Heart

———————◆———————

*You will seek Me and find Me when you search for*
*Me with all your heart.* – Jeremiah 29:13

My wife and I have four beautiful children. Three of them are rambunctious little boys who are full of life and energy. The other is a precious little princess from Uganda whom God allowed to become a part of our forever family through adoption. I love all of my children more than anything in this world. They are priceless gifts to us from the Lord. I love to see them excited about what they are involved in at the moment. There is no prouder father than me.

My sons waste no energy loafing around. Whether it's being super ninjas trying to save the world or professional athletes trying to win the championship, they are always consumed with the task at hand. Oftentimes, one of them will want to show me his latest ability – show off, in other words. It may involve bouncing a soccer ball off of his knee or head. Or it may include learning how to do a flip as he escapes the enemy trying to take his camp. Regardless of the circumstance, their intent is to impress me. No matter how spectacular the stunt or trick, I've seen it before and probably did it myself when I was a little boy.

Simply stated, I am not moved by their ability. However, let one of them fall down, get hurt, or cry out in desperation for Daddy, then they've got my attention. There is not a brick wall sturdy enough to keep me from getting to them in their moment of desperation as they cry out for me. That is the heart of a father coming out to meet the cries of his child.

This epitomizes the church today. We try to impress God with our various abilities. We want Him to be moved by our preaching, singing, buildings, and programs. We think what we can do impresses His heart. Can't you hear Him saying, "You preached a great message, but remember, I wrote the book," or "The worship was great; however, you haven't heard the angelic choir of heaven yet."

We spend more of our time trying to impress God than crying out for Him in desperation. I believe the heart of the heavenly Father is reflected in the heart of the earthly father. He isn't drawn to our tricks or stunts; He is drawn to a heart that is desperate and crying out for Him. We see in the Bible that You will seek Me and find Me when you search for Me with all of your heart (Jeremiah 29:13). We find Him when we seek Him with desperation.

We see this clearly in Scripture as we continue the story of Bartimaeus. After he took a realistic look at where he was, something in his heart changed. At this point, he goes through the second stage of his process of living life more fulfilled than ever.

## STAGE 2: DESPERATION

Bartimaeus had to overcome reality in order to see the big picture of what Jesus could do in and through him. But he needed more than realistic self-evaluation; he had to desire change. This required connecting his mind to his heart. His desperation grew until he put everything on the line in hopes that Jesus would make him new.

Bartimaeus reached his turning point. He became so disgusted with where he was that he became frantic to change. Many churches have a realistic view of where they are, but they never get to the point of desperation. The only thing that separated Bartimaeus from anyone else in that town was his despondency. In that moment of desperation, the change was set in motion.

This new sense of direction from Bartimaeus did not come

> **The critics in your life can be stumbling blocks, or they can be motivation.**

without challenges. We see in the story that the people around him began to discourage him from calling out to Jesus. They did not feel as strongly as Bartimaeus did about what needed to happen. It made no difference to them if his life was changed or not. They criticized him for crying out to the Son of God.

Likewise, pastors must know that when they and their church get desperate enough to change, not everyone will share their desperation. I want to encourage you to resolve in your heart today to do whatever it takes to move forward. The critics in your life can be stumbling blocks, or they can be motivation.

My grandfather, Dr. Jimmy Tharpe, used to say, "I despise those guys who criticize and minimize those vigorous guys whose enterprise helped them rise above those guys who criticize."

This must be true in your heart. Your pain of staying the same has to exceed the pain of changing in order to become desperate enough to move forward. You can do it!

Many in Bartimaeus's situation would have sat back down and let Jesus pass through town simply because they did not want to be opposed. Think about it: His life was moments away from being renewed. He was moments away from seeing colors for the first time. Moments away from having a new perspective on life. Even more significant, he was moments away from meeting Jesus – face to face. In fact, the first face he would ever see would be the One who would later die for him. He could have caved to the pressure, sat down, and let his life waste away. Instead, he pressed forward and experienced the newness of life that only Christ brings.

Desperation is something to which God is drawn. The beginning of desperation means the end of man's abilities. When we can't go any further, we give God the opportunity to be most honored and glorified in our life. At the end of our rope, God is just getting started. Bartimaeus had no other place to go. There was no one else for him to turn to in hopes of having a future different from his past.

Perhaps this is your church today. Maybe you know you need to change. You know that God has great plans for your faith family. You know that you want to move forward, but you're paralyzed by fear of opposition. Put yourself in Bartimaeus's sandals; your life and the life of your church could be refreshed. I challenge you to press forward in desperation for God to move in and through you in unprecedented power.

# CHAPTER 3

# Redeeming the Time:
## Deciding to Sell Out to the Gospel

———⚊———

*And He said to them, 'Follow Me, and I will make*
*you fishers of men.' Immediately they left their nets*
*and followed Him.* – Matthew 4:19-20

O ne of the most memorable times in life comes in the
euphoria of a moment that changes two peoples' lives
forever with a bended knee, a ring, and one simple word: "Yes!"

Of course, this is the beautiful picture of a man and woman
getting engaged. This couple has met along the journey of life.
They have fallen deeply in love, often dreaming about what
life would look like together. This couple has spent many long
hours on the phone exchanging "I love you" endings. They have
cautiously talked about where they would get married, where
they would go on their honeymoon, and even how many children they would have.

This couple has planned out life together before ever actually
committing their lives to each other. They have written their
own fairy-tale story, and these plans remain an object of the
imagination because one thing has yet to happen – he has not
asked her to marry him.

In American culture, it is customary for the man to ask the woman to marry him. Of course, first he must get the blessing of the bride-to-be's father. Should he be lucky enough to get the old affirmative nod from Dad, the man will then buy the ring that will symbolize to the woman he loves that his heart is taken. All that's left is to plan that special time when he will pour his heart out and ask her to come along on the journey of a lifetime, as husband and wife together.

This is that magical moment, the time when all the past seems irrelevant, the present seems frozen, and the future seems hopeful. This is the moment of decision! She must decide to leave her family, her name, and her past, and merge her heart and life with this man for the remaining days of her life.

This moment of decision will define her future. It will place her on a totally new path of life. It will give her a new identity to cling to. She must decide to say yes or no to this man.

Churches today are in the same position. They see the reality of where they are; they become desperate for God to do something new and fresh in them; and now they must make a decision to step forward and trust God for their new direction. We see a parallel of this when we again visit the life of Bartimaeus.

## STAGE 3: DECISION TIME
Of all the amazing things happening that day in Jericho, one astonishing encounter still remained. Bartimaeus succeeded in getting the attention of Jesus. The Son of God in the flesh stopped and called him near. The moment of decision for Bartimaeus had come. He had to decide to stay in his current reality or step out in faith to the call of Christ. This sounds

somewhat simplistic in its context, but this was a critical time for Bartimaeus. In the moment Jesus called out to him, he had to decide whether or not he was all in.

Many churches are at the same crossroads. They must decide if they will stay where they are. Some churches choose to do nothing even when holy restlessness sets in, and some move toward the voice of God calling them. They will either stay where it's safe and comfortable, or they will dare to step out into the unknown because they hear the voice of the Master calling.

This is the decision they must make! Pastors, maybe this is the decision you have been struggling with. Perhaps you know where God is calling you to lead your church, yet the path seems too difficult and uncertain. I encourage you to see the rest of this story before making your decision.

> **He had to decide to stay in his current reality or step out in faith to the call of Christ.**

In a beautiful portrait of a man needing Jesus more than anything else, Bartimaeus jumps up and leaves his cloak, likely one of his prized possessions, behind. He teaches us that nothing in the present state is worth the glorious things that await us when Jesus calls. He exemplifies total surrender of the present circumstance for the hope of the future that Jesus can bring.

Bartimaeus made the decision. He knew that by staying in his situation he would be settling for less than what God wanted for him. He laid it all on the table and decided to be all in. I love his tenacity. He had overcome two major setbacks in life: He had overcome the voices of criticism that literally intended to shout him back down to his lowly place on the ground, and then he made his way to a future he could have never dreamed of.

The story ends well. Bartimaeus receives his sight, and his life is transformed forever. Can you imagine what it must have been like to see colors for the first time in your life? Can you imagine that the first face he ever saw was the Man you and I long to see? Can you imagine the gasps that were heard in the air when Jesus radically changed Bartimaeus? You see, God's plan was for the lives of Jesus and Bartimaeus to intersect and to collide so that God could be glorified through circumstance.

If you are a pastor or church leader, I would like to ask you a few questions. What do you really sense God is saying about where your church is today? Do you sense that God is laying things on your heart to do as a church leader, but you have been hesitant or fearful? What is holding you back from experiencing God's greatest blessings on your church? All these need to be pondered and a decision needs to be made.

As a pastor, I know how hard this is. At times I felt God was leading us to do certain things, yet out of comfort or fear I succumbed to the deception of the enemy. Sometimes I wanted to see certain things done, yet didn't feel like I had the energy to fight the battle to get it done. Though I wanted to walk across the street where Jesus was, I settled for my dusty street corner. Pastor, this kind of submission to the enemy is not the plan of God! Thom Rainer sums it up well in his book Breakout Churches when he says, "It's a sin to be good, when God has called us to be great."[2] This statement from Rainer ushered conviction into my heart as a pastor. God hasn't called us to settle for our dusty street corner. He has called us to life, the abundant life given through Jesus. This is true for individuals and corporately as churches. He has called us to greatness through the power and work of the Holy Spirit.

We have a great task. Time is short. Eternities are at stake! We can no longer sit by on our corner and let the Master pass by. We must take the initiative to get up and move in the direction He is calling us. Like Bartimaeus, we must make a decision to embrace God's plan for our churches.

> **God hasn't called us to settle for our dusty street corner. He has called us to life, the abundant life given through Jesus.**

Pastors, seek God's future for your church before you continue in this book. I challenge you to examine where you are. I pray you would become so desperate for God to move in a bold, fresh way that you would be willing to do anything to see it happen. Today, right now, I pray you would follow hard after the voice of Him who is calling you to leave your safety and comfort and step out into the plans He has for you and your church's future. Obedience doesn't disappoint!

# CHAPTER 4

# A Fatal Attraction:
## Unsuccessfully Pursuing Success

———————

*But seek first His kingdom and His righteousness, and*
*all these things will be added to you.* – Matthew 6:33

Few things in America are as spectacular as the strip in Las Vegas on a clear night. The city's glitz and enchanting, fluorescent illumination can be seen for mile after dusty desert mile. The atmosphere exudes excitement and adventure.

People walk the city streets all night. Endless activities beckon tourists. On almost every corner, casinos promise a chance for a brighter financial future with virtually no effort. Hotels and restaurants give you the opportunity to dine and lounge like a VIP. In this city, commoners brush shoulders with stars. This is Las Vegas!

In the midst of this city that never closes down, you find great deception. The billboards tout fun and excitement. The lure of quick riches abounds. The bells of the wedding chapels are always ringing. But lives are shattered daily in this great city.

Many leave, broke and full of regret. Marriage ceremonies are ample, yet other couples are destroyed by the rampant prostitution and vice. For too many people, the excitement turns into irreversible devastation. Those lights and glamour are full of empty promises.

Unfortunately, there are some parallels to this in church ministry. Many will leave Bible college or seminary chasing the ministerial version of the American dream. It is not as much about money and materials as it is about power, position, popularity, and prestige. We wholeheartedly abandon ourselves to the promise of bigger churches, more staff, greater preaching opportunities, and positions within our denominations or ministry networks.

> **We wholeheartedly abandon ourselves to the promise of bigger churches, more staff, greater preaching opportunities, and positions within our denominations or ministry networks.**

The lure of overnight success and instant notoriety is much like the mesmerizing neon of Las Vegas for these young ministers. They desire to be invited to speak at the next big conference or write the next best-selling book. Bigger, we convince ourselves, is better.

This fatal attraction destroys some great young ministers who could have been significantly useful to the kingdom, but for the draw of the lights and center stage. However, once they buy in to the pursuit of success rather than being faithful to the call that God has placed on their lives, often it's too late. The deception of the attraction births something in their hearts that cannot be spiritually satisfied, because it's driven by the flesh.

I experienced this as a younger minister. I believed that I had to preach a certain way, or more aptly, not preach a certain way or risk not growing our church. I gave in somewhat to the pursuit of what is too often deemed pastoral success.

There came a point where I found myself studying the way other people who had become "successful" in ministry preached. I would imitate those men instead of exercising the uniqueness that God gave to me. I wanted nothing more than to be the next "big deal" in my profession.

But pursuing this attraction involved being something God did not design me to be. He revealed this in my heart and rescued me from the pitfalls of my own selfish desires. This is the attraction of modern-day ministry, to do whatever it takes to be on top.

But we do not find this in the Bible. In fact, Jesus taught just the opposite. He taught us to be last, not first. His teachings were aimed to move us into the background, not center stage. Jesus instructed people not to tell what He had

> **In our consumer-saturated culture, the church has created this monster of ministerial ego that can only be fed by the sinful desire of self-advancement.**

done so He could stay out of the spotlight. However, in our consumer-saturated culture, the church has created this monster of ministerial ego that can only be fed by the sinful desire of self-advancement. Anything or anyone that gets in its way usually ends up devastated and deeply wounded.

So what should God's view of success look like for us today? Scripture gives us a great example of how to live out our lives and ministries in a way that is kingdom-focused instead of self-focused or ego-driven. This example teaches both humility and networking (used here to describe sanctified relationship building and maintaining to distinguish it from the world's definition of networking) for kingdom purposes. We find it in the story of Andrew.

Andrew had established himself as a follower and disciple of John the Baptist. He was devoted to John's teaching and followed him daily. However, the moment John described Jesus as the Lamb of God who takes away our sins, something turned Andrew's heart. He immediately left to follow Jesus.

Andrew knew what John was implying, and he was wise enough to leave what was good (John) for what was best (Jesus). However, along the way, Andrew became burdened for his brother Simon, who would later be called Peter. Andrew went and told his brother that he had found the long-awaited Messiah and brought Simon to meet Jesus.

I'm sure Andrew would have never imagined what would happen next. In the exchange between Simon and Jesus, an anointing happened. Simon became Peter, and Jesus called him out, blessed him, and anointed his future (John 1:42). Right before Andrew's eyes, Peter was called into a life of ministry and ultimately death for the faith he would live out.

So what about Andrew? He is the one who introduced Peter to Jesus. He is the one who used his networking ability to further the kingdom. He is the one who influenced Peter to be an influencer for the gospel. But you will never see his name on the marquee sign or the spotlight on his life and preaching. Yet Andrew is the hero here.

This is a great example for all of us of how Jesus can use us in unimaginable ways if we are more focused on people and the kingdom than our own advancement and agenda. Andrew could have pitched a fit in front of Jesus when he was not the anointed one. He could have become bitter and resentful toward Peter throughout his life when Peter would seemingly be more successful. He could have scolded Jesus about how unfair he believed it was that Peter would be the main influencer in the beginning of the organized church, but that's not Andrew.

Andrew was not enamored by success and spotlights. He was simply faithful to the call that Jesus had given him. In fact, we don't find anything in the Scriptures that would indicate that Andrew ever felt the sting of jealousy.

We need more men like Andrew, who are more drawn to being faithful to the call, than being drawn to man-centered ministerial success. I have often heard men say that their list of friends who began ministry with them shrunk each year

> **We need more men like Andrew, who are more drawn to being faithful to the call, than being drawn to man-centered ministerial success.**

as more of those names would drop off the list due to acts of immorality, burnout, pressure, and other reasons.

Most of the men that I have heard say these things will also tell you there were names on that list of men who are no longer in ministry because they had a superstar mindset. They had visions of being the next Billy Graham or the youngest mega-church pastor in the nation. This often led to pride, which we know ultimately will destroy any minister of God.

So what does Andrew teach us about pursuing faithfulness instead of self-gratifying success in ministry? We can see a clear picture in Andrew's life that can help us ensure we are walking with our heart and mind aligned to make Jesus known.

## THE SECOND-MAN PRINCIPLE

Andrew teaches us a valuable life lesson on what it means to be the second man. He was second man to John the Baptist. When Jesus burst onto the scene, he became the second man to Him. To top it off, he introduces Peter to Jesus and once again takes the second-man position.

When speaking of the second-man principle, I am not talking about power or position. I am describing more of a background role. He is not the one on the stage under the lights, but he is a part of the production.

My wife and I recently attended a Christian music concert. The place was packed with thousands of people, and the atmosphere was electric. There were two major artists performing before the crowd. The songs they were singing were just a small part of the concert experience. Many lights and screens complemented the emotion of the moment.

The artists were on the stage, lit up by the spotlights, but they were not the only ones in the show. Behind the stage were many people dressed in black who were responsible for every other aspect of the concert except the singing. While the artists were the center of attention, the stagehands were just as essential to the experience.

This is what Andrew spent his life doing. He was the second man, the one who would network so everything else would click into place. Though he was not the center of attention, he was as influential as anyone else because of his kingdom-networking abilities.

As ministers, we must learn to be content being the second man. John the Baptist spells this out for us when he says, He [Jesus] must increase, but I must decrease (John 3:30). Any minister should know that he will need to spend his life being the second man to Jesus. This sounds so simple, yet many ministers draw attention to themselves instead of to Jesus.

There must be a frequent, gut-wrenching heart check in our ministries. We must check our pride and selfishness at the door when choosing to follow the call of Jesus in ministry. We must be certain that we are in ministry for all the right reasons.

As a minister, it's useful to look at where you are and how you got there. You should be able to reflect on your journey and see God's hand in any move you have made. This is not always the case. My wife and I spent almost a year in Tennessee because I forced a move to chase a good idea instead of a God idea. These things happen when you are focused more on your future than on God's future for you.

Pastors and church leaders, God has a great plan for you in His kingdom. He desires to use you more than you can even imagine. I implore you today to learn how to live off of center stage, to bow out, and let Jesus be the star. He can do more through you than you could ever do on your own.

I also pray that you will not fall into the deception of ministerial stardom. There will be many things that attract you: bigger churches, larger buildings, and lucrative salaries could end up being great thorns of temptation in your flesh. You will be approached by people wanting to show you greener grass. In these cases, I hope you will remember Andrew and choose faithfulness over a false sense of success.

# CHAPTER 5

# Dying to Grow:
## Debunking the Myths of Ministry

———————◆———————

*Trust in the LORD and do good; Dwell in the land
and cultivate faithfulness.* – Psalm 37:3

I love my wife! She is the apple of my eye. I will never forget
the moment when those doors swung open and she began
to walk down that aisle to become my wife. I have never seen
a more beautiful woman, shining in all of her glory. A few
moments later, we exchanged vows, and she became my wife;
we promised to remain united until death separates us. That
was our wedding day, the best day of my life.

Of course, that was the easy part. The process of two becoming one flesh, as the Bible says in Genesis 2, was a much more
difficult process. We enjoy a strong, healthy marriage, but it's
not always easy. We had to learn about each other and our daily
routines. We had to respect each other's values and traditions,
poured into us by our families, while trying to figure out who
we were going to be together. We had to learn how to compro-
mise and do life together as a couple and a family.

The most difficult thing in marriage most couples face is
overcoming unrealistic expectations. We all have an idea of

what marriage should be. We have been told things about marriage that we presuppose will be true in our own. We dream of how we will live happily ever after. Yet many couples fail to realize that many of the things they are told and taught, and have come to believe, are simply myths.

These myths exist in ministry today. Many ministers have an idea of what a life of ministry is supposed to look like, but get into it and are rattled with reality. They dream of who they want to be and end up abandoning the call to pursue their dream. The problem is that often the dreams are unrealistic myths that have been passed down through the generations.

> **In the pursuit of growing, we are actually dying because we are forsaking the Great Commission.**

These myths can be the downfall of ministers, even those who are extremely gifted. On the journey of chasing these unrealistic milestones, the very heart of God is replaced with selfish ambition. The mission of reaching the world for Christ is replaced with attaining the fastest-growing church. In the pursuit of growing, we are actually dying because we are forsaking the Great Commission.

The church we see in Acts saw dramatic growth on a daily basis because evangelism was at its core. They were not interested in the rock-star culture of ministry that we have today. They were more interested in seeing lives transformed by the power of the gospel than in filling any kind of building with people. It was driven by the gospel, not by myths that we believe establish our success.

We can identify and debunk four major myths we see in ministry today:

## MYTH 1: I WILL BE SUCCESSFUL IF MY CHURCH IS LARGE

Let's be honest. This is the dream locked away in the heart of most pastors as they start out in ministry. We want to lead mega-churches with lots of people, resources, and influence. Who wouldn't want that? Unfortunately, many young ministers become obsessed with this goal and let it become their main motivation. This is not God's heart for the minister.

**We must remember that God is not impressed by us in the slightest, but He is pleased with us when we rest in His calling.**

God's desire for the minister is to be faithful to the field that he is called to. You won't find in the Bible where God places in man a selfishness that causes him to abandon the very purpose for his ministry. That is sin creeping into the life of a minister and robbing him of the joy of representing God.

If your motivation is to pastor a large church, you are missing the point of what God called you to. He called you to a life of serving Him. Granted, many will pastor large churches and do well. I am not implying that large-church pastors did anything apart from being faithful to the call to get where they are. In fact, God gifts many with the leadership, administration, and ability to pastor large churches. I am simply pointing out that our motivation must be to be faithful to the call of God and to the gospel and let God strategically place us where He wants us.

Ministering to a large church does not make you successful; being faithful wherever God has planted you does. That
could be a small, rural church or an urban mega-church. It
doesn't matter as long as you are where God has placed you.
We must measure success through God's eyes and not primarily by numbers of people or campuses that we have. We must
remember that God is not impressed by us in the slightest, but
He is pleased with us when we rest in His calling.

## MYTH 2: IT'S ABOUT WHO YOU KNOW

Networking merely to get to know the right people and get into
the right places is an easy trap to fall into. That mindset can
lead to the advancement of our own kingdom, not God's. Kingdom advancement is about promoting and glorifying God,
not self.

> **We must depend on the Holy Spirit to do the work in and through us more than we depend on our connections with others.**

I believe in and love networking with people who add
value to the kingdom. I think it
is essential in helping us fulfill
the Great Commission. But networking should be driven by the
desire to do more for His kingdom or to help others much more
than it should be to benefit us. When we fall to the deception
that we must know people in order to advance, we sell short
the power of the Holy Spirit in our lives.

The Holy Spirit does use people we know to lead us where
God wants us. In fact, that's the beauty of having relation-
ships in ministry, allowing the Spirit to use us to help others.
However, we must depend on the Holy Spirit to do the work

in and through us more than we depend on our connections with others.

It is also important to realize we may know people who can help us, but it doesn't necessarily mean that help is from God. We can listen to the voices of people who love us and want what's best for us, but they may not know what God knows. We must rely on knowing the Holy Spirit in our life and ministry. He is the only One who can truly lead us to be in the center of God's will.

## MYTH 3: IF MY CHURCH IS GROWING IT MUST BE HEALTHY

One of the greatest misconceptions in the ministry world today is that we equate growth with health. We love to tell people that our church is rapidly growing. We love to go to meetings or conferences and talk about our space and parking issues. We experience a great sense of pride when we are able to proclaim that we are adding a service to our schedule. All of these things put off a great feeling in our hearts. Yet it is important to note that not everything that grows is healthy.

We tend to think that only things that are vibrant and healthy grow. Children grow to be strong and healthy. Fruit trees grow tall and produce great treats. We hope that our bank accounts grow and give us the retirement we all dream of having. All of these would be good types of growth and things to celebrate.

But there are unhealthy things that grow also. A tumor in your body will grow and could be terminal. In the midst of a beautiful spring flower bed, weeds can grow and choke out your colorful creation. This simply teaches us that all things that are getting bigger are not necessarily getting better.

This was the case in a church that I pastored. Things looked great and many people were coming. We had become the exciting church in the area. We were the church people were talking about, and people left their own churches to come be a part of ours. This was fun and rapid growth, but it was not healthy growth. We were growing by transfer more than we were by transformation. We decided to change our mindset and began to see healthy growth due to people coming to faith in Christ. It was a slower growth, but it looked more like what we see in the book of Acts.

Of course, many churches that are growing are healthy. They are doing the right things in order to draw people into their fellowship. They have evangelism at the core of their strategy, which in return will produce health.

Churches that are growing by numbers, services, campuses, and other measurements must be certain that the growth is a healthy form, having the mission of Jesus in their strategy to reach the lost with the message of the cross. This is the ultimate producer of health and vitality in any culture or denomination. We must have evangelism as the fuel that drives the growth of our churches.

## MYTH 4: WE MUST MIRROR CULTURE TO CHANGE CULTURE

One of the greatest tragedies that can be identified today is the lack of distinction between the church and culture. Many churches and leaders take the mindset that in order to engage culture, the church must embrace culture. Therefore, their strategies make the gospel less intentional and more relational.

In time, the church begins to look more like the culture than different from the culture.

Some pastors believe the myth that the only way to reach people is to go do what the people do. I am a proponent of reaching the lost in every place, but not at the cost of integrity and holiness. I have seen many pastors engage in things that they once held convictions about, just so they could share the gospel. Remember, Jesus embraced sinners, but he never engaged in the sin to reach them.

> If evangelism is really in our DNA, we cannot mimic the culture. We must be lights to a dark and lonely world. In falling for this myth, we risk distorting the gospel.

The church is called to be different, to stand out in our society. Jesus tells us that we are the light of the world (Matthew 5:14). Light and darkness cannot share space, and neither can holiness and sinfulness.

As ministers, we must reject the lie that we must look like the lost in order to reach them. If evangelism is really in our DNA, we cannot mimic the culture. We must be lights to a dark and lonely world. In falling for this myth, we risk distorting the gospel.

In the culture of ministry, there will always be easy ways to grow your church. They will be written about in books, taught at conferences, and sold as models. However, it is imperative that we keep our eyes on Jesus to remain faithful to His calling for our lives.

# CHAPTER 6

# Overcoming the Critic:

## Prevailing amid People with the Spiritual Gift of Criticism

———————⚓———————

*Finally, brethren, whatever is true, whatever is*
*honorable, whatever is right, whatever is pure,*
*whatever is lovely, whatever is of good repute, if there*
*is any excellence and if anything worthy of praise,*
*dwell on these things. –* Philippians 4:8

About midsummer, the anticipation starts to build for a game played on an oblong field with an inflated pigskin. The game of football is both captivating and inspiring. I love watching the culmination of commitment, sacrifice, and sheer determination play itself out for four quarters on the gridiron.

In every game I watch, I choose a team that I want to win. I cheer this team on in the comfort of my living room, as if I am three rows up on the fifty-yard line. I get excited when they get a much-needed first down. I jump up and yell when they miss a tackle for a loss. I won't even tell you what I do when my team scores a touchdown!

Yet there is one other thing I do as a spectator, as one who hasn't put in the time and effort to have a legitimate voice in the game. I criticize! Yep, right from my couch, I tell the coach how bad the play he called was. I yell at the television, asking the coach, "What were you thinking?" In my mind, I know better than the coach who has studied the opposing team, prepared his men for battle, and lost sleep over developing the right strategy to win the game. I am a Monday-morning armchair quarterback who is critical about things I really shouldn't be.

A great parallel exists between who I am on Saturdays in the fall and how people in the church are on a weekly basis. The pastor has studied the Scriptures and the culture and developed a strategy to reach his community for Christ; yet voices of criticism ring in his mind. He is the one who has spent hours pouring over what it is that God wants him to say to the church. He is the one who has lost sleep over making the best decisions for the future of the church. He is the one who has been given the responsibility to coach the team that we know to be a congregation, knowing that with every step he takes, armchair quarterbacks are awaiting an opportunity to ask, "What were you thinking?"

Few things can hinder a great vision from becoming a success faster than unnecessary criticism. This disapproving analysis has a devastating power to distract a leader from doing what God has called him to do. Criticism can cause a leader to doubt his calling and ability and, therefore, can result in a church's demise. Unwarranted and unnecessary criticisms are tools in the enemy's toolbox.

When I was pursuing my education, no one ever taught me how to deal with criticism as a pastor. I was unaware of the reality that pastors are under constant scrutiny from someone nearly all the time. I had to learn this on the job. I knew how to develop a sermon, perform a wedding, administer the Lord's Supper, but not how to deal with criticism.

The pastor who can't handle criticism is in great danger. Negative criticism has more potential to destroy the pastor and his family than any other pitfall of ministry. If he's not careful, the pastor spends all his time handling everyone else's problems and responding to every last criticism. This weighs on his heart and mind and will overflow into his family.

Unfortunately, criticism is a fixture for the minister, being one of those occupational hazards of the job. The criticism will not shape the pastor or his ministry; how he handles it will. If a pastor can navigate through the waters of criticism and see it objectively, learning from valid criticism and dismissing that which is not true or valid, he can become a better man and minister as a result.

> **Negative criticism has more potential to destroy the pastor and his family than any other pitfall of ministry.**

Criticism for the leader is not a new phenomenon. It is an ancient challenge that leaders from the beginning of time have dealt with. Many men in the Bible are known for their victories by leading through criticism. One such man was Moses.

Moses was a leader. God had a great plan for Moses that would take him down roads of great criticism and difficulties, as well as numerous God-sized victories. He became a high-level leader who learned to overcome criticism and adversity to see God do incredible things in his lifetime.

The people whom God tasked Moses to lead were high-maintenance people. They were complaining about their circumstances and doubting God's provision, on top of calling Moses' leadership into question. Despite their hearts' condition, Moses loved these people and wanted nothing more than to lead them into the land of promise.

The leadership of Moses had its ups and downs, but whose doesn't? He led hard and well, never giving up on the vision God had spoken to him. In Numbers 12, we see some valuable principles from Moses that help us learn how to lead through the dark days of criticism.

God used Moses' conviction along the journey to introduce him to a young lady by the name of Zipporah. His heart would fall in love with her, and she would become his wife. The only problem was that she was a Cushite woman from Midian. This didn't sit too well with Moses' brother and sister. They were not happy with the bride of his choice. Their discontentment spewed out, and they soon became a choir of chronic complainers. Moses had to decide to lead through the criticism or bow out. He led on, providing an example for us in overcoming criticism.

## OVERCOMING JEALOUSY

Aaron and Miriam were jealous. They could not stand the fact that God was using their brother Moses to lead Israel. They wanted to be a part of the leadership. They wanted their time in the spotlight. This exposing of their hearts shows us that they were not happy for Moses, but envious of him.

This duo began to plant seeds of doubt concerning Moses' leadership. They did everything they could to cast the light upon themselves. They began to compare what God was doing in them versus what He was doing in Moses. This could have created a real problem for the Israelite people who had already endured so much. However, God was in Moses' corner.

This story is so applicable in many lives and churches. People doing what they should do and leading well are facing extreme jealousy and opposition. Pastor, you will face jealous people in your ministry. These people will seek to tear you down and sow seeds of doubt in others' minds about your leadership. Follow the lead of Moses and allow God, who called you to lead, to defend you.

Moses could have responded. He could have fired right back with words that would later haunt him. Yet Moses chose not to fight the battle of ungodly envy. He remained focused on the calling that God had given him – to lead the people well. This is to be our response as well – to rest in the certainty of God's calling instead of dwelling in the land of envy.

## REMAINING FAITHFUL

Moses knew the task at hand. He had heard from the Lord about what to do with His people. His greatest hurdle was to lead these people day in and day out to the Promised Land, while at the same time leading them to trust God for their every need. As if this wasn't enough, he was continuously under scrutiny and criticism.

Moses' life was not marked by tangible measures of success. In fact, he never even had the chance to step foot in the Promised Land himself. He would look down from the edge of the mountain to see the land that he dreamed of for all these years, but was not granted access by the Lord.

Sure, he will always be remembered for crossing the Red Sea. He will always be tagged in relationship with the Ten Commandments. His life will always be honored as the one led by a cloud in the day and fire at night. He will go down in history as the only man who ever had a conversation with God in the form of a burning bush. But none of these match God's characterization of Moses.

God saw Moses as humble and faithful. In God's response to Aaron and Miriam, He chose to lay out who Moses was, not what he had done. God could have given a long list of things Moses had accomplished with His help. Instead, He chose to point out the person of Moses, not his performance.

Pastors, this is a great example for us. We must stay focused on the vision to which God has called us and remain humble and faithful. Moses could have gone back to his tent discouraged and depressed. He could have begun to nurture the seeds of doubt that were being planted in the shallow soil of his mind. He could have walked away and decided to do something else with his life. But God calls him faithful.

He was faithful to the call that God placed on his life, to the people God called him to lead, and to the vision that was set before him. What could have been a distraction gave Moses more determination. Likewise, the pastor must concentrate on being faithful and not consumed with the criticisms thrown his way. He is God's called man. The faithful pastor has God in his corner!

## PRAYING FOR YOUR OFFENDERS

Perhaps one of the greatest lessons we can learn from Moses' life is when Moses had been brought through the wringer by his own family. Of all the people who could criticize him, his family leveled insults. This did not please God. Moses had been humble and faithful to the Lord, and his brother and sister were in trouble. In God's displeasure with Miriam and her attitude toward Moses, He turned her into a leper.

Can you imagine what Moses felt? He had tried to remain focused and drown out the words of these two critics. Suddenly, the Lord intervened and Moses' sister became an outcast, stricken by the consequences of displeasing God. Miriam and Aaron quickly realized their grand mistake.

> **The pastor must concentrate on being faithful and not consumed with the criticisms thrown his way. He is God's called man. The faithful pastor has God in his corner!**

Let's be honest. How many of us would have celebrated the wrath of God coming down upon our critics? We would likely have said something to the effect of, "That's what you get for messing with God's man." This was not the heart of Moses. He was broken over the discipline of his sister. As much as her criticisms hurt, he could not bear to see her in this condition. So Moses did what made him so great a leader in the first place; he prayed for God to heal her.

Moses was more concerned about who she was than what she said. He knew that her words about him were unwarranted and came from a heart that was hurting. His heart was for her heart to be right with God. He hurt knowing she was enduring the consequences of her sin.

What if we led this way? What if people who were our offenders or greatest critics found grace in us instead of retaliation? We must be proactive in praying for our critics instead of reactive to their often-unwarranted charges. God chose Moses because he knew Moses' heart was for his people, not his personal gain.

At times, we fail at this. There are times when we feel as if the whole world is coming against us. In these moments, we will not objectively see God's hand moving. We will instead listen and be consumed with comments that people make. In these moments, the greatest position of strength is found on our knees, praying for our critics.

If you are a leader, you will have to endure people who neither like you nor follow you. It is a daily struggle to remain focused while trying to understand the reasons for the criticism you are getting. Let me remind you: Moses' only response was to pray for Miriam. He didn't retaliate. He didn't take joy in her affliction. He loved her and prayed for her, a characteristic that would reflect God's favor upon his life.

# CHAPTER 7

# A Conversation with God:

## Leading Your Church to Pray for the Lost

———————— ·— ————————

*Brethren, my heart's desire and my prayer to God
for them is for their salvation.* – Romans 10:1

H as it ever occurred to you that the reason we are not seeing
people come to faith in Jesus, as we know we should, is
because we aren't praying for them?

We might spend time praying for our churches to grow. We
lift up the sick to our heavenly Father. But can you recall the last
time you joined with a local church body in a corporate prayer
time pleading specifically for
those headed toward an eternity separated from God?

Ministers ask each other
why people aren't responding
to the gospel message. They
study and prepare all week long, awaiting the time to preach
the gospel, only to go home each week dejected and discouraged
at the lack of response. Perhaps it's not a sermon problem or a
preaching problem. Maybe it's a praying problem.

> **Perhaps it's not a sermon
> problem or a preaching
> problem. Maybe it's a
> praying problem.**

Throughout the New Testament is this model of praying for people to hear the gospel. In Romans 10, Paul says, Brethren, my heart's desire and my prayer to God for them is for their salvation (Romans 10:1). We sense Paul's heart for the lost. He desperately wants to see the Gentiles come to a saving knowledge of Jesus. He writes to the church in Rome that he is praying for their salvation. Paul is modeling a heart of praying for the lost.

In Colossians 4:3, we see Paul pleading with the church to pray for the gospel to go forth. He writes, praying at the same time for us as well, that God will open up to us a door for the word, so that we may speak forth the mystery of Christ. This writing doesn't just inspire us to pray for the lost. It also helps us recognize that we should adopt a heart like Paul's. Though imprisoned, he was offering up prayers for

> **I would rather offend someone in the hope that they might gain heaven than ignore them on their way to hell.**

those who crossed his path and for many whom he'd never met. We need to get on our faces and daily plead for those who are living hopelessly.

As ministers, we should be the first to exemplify this to our people. We should have a running list of lost people whom we are praying for. We should remind our church of this list and ask them to add names to the list. Many churches have a midweek prayer meeting. Typically, in this meeting, the people on this list are discussed much more than they're prayed for. In most churches, the health issues portion of the list will be much longer than the salvation list. People are sometimes afraid that they may offend a person by putting them on the list for salvation if word were to get back to them. Honestly, most believers are tactful enough not to divulge such things to those on the outside. Nonetheless, I would rather offend someone in the hope that they might gain heaven than ignore them on their way to hell. Their eternity is at risk. We must identify and pray for them.

If churches could ever convince their people to pray for the lost, their burden for the lost would be recaptured, and lost friends, relatives, and even strangers would be the benefactors as the gospel would be shared out of the overflow of God's inner working. Oh, that we could capture the heart of Paul for the lost and make it a priority to pray for them.

One of my greatest experiences in a church came through prayer. I felt the Lord wanted us as a church to pray for two weeks during our services. Instead of me preaching to them, we prayed to Him! We called it a prayer summit, actually stopping the routine schedule of our worship services and going before the Lord in prayer. God amazed us in what He did through that time in our church. I can only imagine what God would do in our churches across the world if we would stop our routines and start praying.

When praying for the lost, we must pray specifically. We need to ask the Lord for our lost friends' salvation by name. Sure, God already knows who they are and the condition of their hearts. He knows that they have not surrendered to Him. Even so, this gives us the opportunity to lift their names before Him on behalf of their souls. We should daily pray for these friends and loved ones by name, asking God to use us in their conversion.

We should also pray for the unconverted in our circle of influence. There are many people who pray for others for many years before they come to faith in Jesus. That same consistency must drive us to the Father daily, begging for the souls of our acquaintances. Of course, we may never see in our lifetime the outcome of our prayers. But one day, we'll rejoice and eternally celebrate with some of those whom we prayed for.

Another thing we should do in praying for the lost is to pray expectantly. When we pray for a lost friend, we should do so expecting the Lord to answer. Mark 11:24 says, all things for which you pray and ask, believe that you have received them, and they will be granted you. We know that this is praying according to God's will. Why pray for the lost if we do not expect God to give the person the opportunity to embrace Him?

God operates in His sovereignty, so we should operate with faith in His sovereignty. God desires for men to come to faith in His Son, so we should believe that we can be used by Him in the process. We must pray expecting God to work in and through us so that He may be glorified by us.

So what does praying for the lost look like practically in our lives and churches? It begins with a heart for the lost and setting aside times of intentional prayer. If you prioritize this time in your church, your people will be more likely to prioritize it in their lives. There are three areas of salvific praying that will help you and your people in this process.

## AWAKENING

In Ecclesiastes 3:11, we come to understand that God has set eternity in the hearts of men. That is, every man has a void that must be filled. This void, what Pascal called a "God-shaped vacuum" inside us, drives us from our first breath to pursue the source of fulfillment and meaning. As Christians, we know that Jesus is the only way to fill such a void. However, the lost person does not know this and is on a journey exploring different things, desperately trying to fill their void.

This powerful, universal truth should spark us to pray that God awakens their hearts to seek Him. We know that deep in their hearts they long for what only Jesus can give. We hold the antidote. Therefore, we must pray for God to awaken the hunger inside of them and that they would turn to Him to be filled.

## REALIZATION

Not only should we pray that God awakens the longing for the eternal in the hearts of the lost, but we should also pray that they realize their great need for a Savior and desire Him. Romans 3:23 tells us, for all have sinned and fall short of the glory of God. We must pray that God would open the eyes of the lost to realize that they are rebellious sinners. We must understand as believers that a person who is unredeemed might not understand that He is the way. Some have never heard. Others have never surrendered. This gives us the opportunity to pray for them to attain a hunger for Jesus and His saving power.

## OPPORTUNITY

If a lost person is to come to faith in Christ, he or she needs to hear the gospel. This will only happen if we pray for God to give them the opportunity to hear the good news. Romans 10:14 says, How then will they call on Him in whom they have not believed? How will they believe in Him whom they have not heard? And how will they hear without a preacher? Clearly, someone must be sharing for the lost to hear.

One of the great things about praying this way for the lost is that God will inevitably burden the hearts of those who are praying to be the ones sharing the gospel. This gives way to believers becoming intentional about the gospel message. They never know if they may be the one who is an answer to someone else's prayer.

What if your church and mine were praying earnestly, expectantly for the lost? Paul models this type of heart for us. The Bible gives us numerous examples of why we should pray expectantly for those without Christ. We must get burdened to lift their names to the Father. When believers turn up the heat in prayer for the lost, God will respond in kind.

CHAPTER 8

# The Rifle Factor:
## Bringing the Gospel into Focus

———————— ⚓ ————————

*For I determined to know nothing among you except*
*Jesus Christ, and Him crucified. – 1 Corinthians 2:2*

I enjoy few things more than watching the sun rise or set while
hunting. Hunting is one of those activities you can do with
your children that provides built-in quality time, and I love that.
It is fun, adventurous, and a great way to provide food for the
family. But going to the woods in camouflage is only part of the
sport. Every good hunter knows you will eventually need a gun.

Choosing between a shotgun or a rifle depends on what type
of animal you're hunting. There is, however, a great difference
between these two. A shotgun is typically used for small, speedy
animals, such as ducks, within a shooting range of fifty yards
or less. You use a shotgun when you're hunting ducks because
the ammunition is released in a spray pattern. At the right distance, this allows the small pellets to spread out and give you
more of a chance to hit the duck, which is usually on the fly.

A rifle, on the other hand, requires precision when aiming
at an animal. The hunter will have a scope attached to the rifle,
which has crosshairs that guide the hunter's aim. Once the trig-

ger is pulled, the bullet will go to the exact point of aim and is capable of traveling hundreds of yards with deadly precision.

Did you get the visual here? A shotgun shell's spray is relative to the direction you aimed the shotgun and imprecise after just a few yards. On the other hand, when aimed correctly, a rifle will place the head of a bullet on the intended target every time. This gives us a great picture of where we are in the church and what we need to do in the future.

As we look toward a practical shifting of mindset and methodology regarding evangelism, we must decide to take the rifle approach and leave the shotgun behind. Too many churches have been trying to accomplish an evangelism ministry, but their efforts are more shotgun than rifle: imprecise, scattered, and unfocused.

> **Too many churches have been trying to accomplish an evangelism ministry, but their efforts are more shotgun than rifle: imprecise, scattered, and unfocused.**

What we need are focused and precise efforts to share our faith and transform our communities. We must center our crosshairs on our cities, using the gospel as ammunition. We must, like a rifleman, aim the gospel with the right approach.

The gospel was never intended to take a backseat to anything. It wasn't intended to be a by-product of church growth. It was to be the primary means of church growth. In Acts, we see the church thriving, but not because of a clever sermon series. It wasn't experiencing unprecedented growth due to location. The music wasn't a draw either. The church grew because it was centered on the only thing that can truly change lives – the gospel.

Churches today are really good at connecting with people. We do everything we can to customize a church "experience" for a guest. We wring our hands in fear that a guest will show up on our church doorstep, but isn't interested in the programs we offer. This is our mindset, to have a buffet of options for everyone.

Programs are good for the church and the attendee. They are a good way to involve guests as well. But too often programs fuel the church rather than the gospel. Sure, traces of the gospel can be found in many of the programs we offer. Some may even have the gospel as their stated reason for existence. Yet many programs are more like the spray from a shotgun, fired by pastors and staff in hopes of grazing the on-the-move, hundred-miles-an-hour churchgoer. This won't do. We must be driven by nothing less than Christ and His gospel.

A church that becomes driven by programs is not a healthy church. In fact, a church that is fueled by anything other than the gospel will become encumbered with the busyness of attracting people rather than reaching people. In its pursuit of growth, it will die.

I am not anti-program. I believe some programs are useful in helping a church get the gospel into the community. But I confess that I have been guilty many times of allowing some sort of visitation, Bible study, or youth event become the check mark on my to-do list. This programmatic approach often led me to staleness rather than vitality. At times I thought to myself, "I've spent enough time at church this week." Rather than seizing a moment of opportunity to minister, in my own self-righteousness the gospel became a duty instead of a privilege.

This happens when churches and individuals spread themselves thin with good activities. They become like that shotgun, still firing and making noise, but only hoping to be effective. We need to become a rifle, precise and accurate. We need to bring the gospel back into focus as the center of everything we do in our churches. This can happen if three simple principles are heeded.

## MAKE ETERNITY YOUR MOTIVATION

When you look at everything you and your church are investing time, resources, and people into, what is your reasoning? It's easy to say we do everything in order for people to hear the gospel; yet this is not always true.

If you are pastoring a well-established church, odds are that you would be stretching it to say everything is for the kingdom's advancement. Let me illustrate for you. I remember a group of senior adult women, sweet as could be, in the first church I pastored. They loved and supported me as if I were one of their grandsons. To be honest, at twenty-three years of age, I could have been. They met religiously every week to make magnificent quilts together.

This ministry among themselves was also somewhat of a program, a ritual that took place at the same time in the church each week, with good fellowship and conversation. They served tasty food and they had a pleasant time each week. These gatherings provided personal encouragement and fellowship.

But sharing the gospel was not a part of the routine or plans.

If I would have had any wisdom at that age as a pastor, I would have encouraged these women to think about their friends who could sew and needed to hear about Jesus. Simply stated, I would have challenged them to become sowers of the gospel while at the same time being sewers of quilts.

I challenge you to take a look at all the things you and your church do and find the motivation for each thing. You may find many things that keep you and your people busy but that are not aiming at the gospel. However, if we can begin to examine everything we do through an eternal lens, we will see more people saved as a result.

## BECOME INTENTIONAL IN EVERYTHING YOU DO

Intentionality is often lacking in our ministries. The default position is a passive approach to our mission. If someone is converted, it's despite such a ministry, not because of it.

Intentionality takes hard work and dedication, causing one to constantly be thinking of ways to improve. Many churches take a come-and-see mentality. We find it easier to do everything we can to attract people to our churches and programs than to go out and connect

> **I was shocked to see that for two years I led this church down a road aimed at attraction rather than transformation.**

with people where they are. This corner-cutting is dangerous because it will create apathy and laziness among God's people.

I know firsthand. A church I pastored was growing but not the way it should have been. We hosted attractive events. We did the necessary things to get people to come. But few people were being transformed. So we made a significant change.

I evaluated every event we did as a church. I was shocked to see that for two years I led this church down a road aimed at attraction rather than transformation. Every event we did was to draw people to our campus. We were sending the message that you must come to our campus to experience what God could do for you.

This new truth cut me to the core. My heart hurt deep within as I realized my misdirection. This wake-up call changed the future of my ministry as their pastor. I became intentional and led my church to become intentionally minded people.

## THE CHANGE-UP

We began to plan most things off campus in order to meet people where they were. We wanted people to know we were willing to come into their lives and settings, just as Jesus was willing to meet them where they were.

I wish I could tell you we tripled in size. We grew slowly, but in a healthy manner. We did, however, grow rapidly in influence and trustworthiness. That is the end result of intentionality and right priority. You gain people's trust, respect, and the opportunity to take the gospel to them right where they are.

## STAY PRACTICAL IN YOUR APPROACH

A frequent mistake I see today is making the gospel message complicated. This goes both for the lost and the churched. We have taken the gospel and made a monster out of it. People are afraid to share the gospel because we have taught them not to mess it up.

This is unfortunate because the gospel is one of the simplest stories to ever grace the lips of humanity. In talking about false conversions or watering down the gospel, we have scared people. They think that if they miss a point in their gospel presentation or don't lead the person to pray a certain prayer in a certain way, they might "mess up" God's work of regeneration in a receptive soul. The message believers need to hear is that God uses willing hearts who will share the reason for the hope they have. Salvation is God's part; testifying to the simple gospel is our high calling.

Remember, Paul said that he brought simplicity with the gospel:

> *And when I came to you, brethren, I did not come with superiority of speech or of wisdom, proclaiming to you the testimony of God. For I determined to know nothing among you except Jesus Christ, and Him crucified. I was with you in weakness and in fear and in much trembling, and my message and my preaching were not in persuasive words of wisdom, but in demonstration of the Spirit and of power, so that your faith would not rest on the wisdom of men, but on the power of God* (1 Corinthians 2:1-5).

This was the heart of Paul, simplicity and practicality in his preaching of the gospel. Of course, the gospel contains deep theological concepts. As preachers, we must remain true to those depths. But we must remind ourselves to see the power in the simplicity of Jesus' message spoken through common words and not to be blinded by our theological astuteness. We must remain practical in our approach in preaching and ministry.

Pastors, I know that you love the Hebrew and Greek languages and study them for hours. I am mesmerized by the power of God's Word when I learn a new truth from the ancient language. But remember that most of the people God places in your path, those soldiers of the cross in your care, will have taken no language studies. We must be able to help them see that they can live out the gospel in their communities practically and powerfully. I

> **You are trying to reach lost people who don't care about the kind of music you sing or which version of the Bible you use.**

would imagine that when they grasp this, the fire to know more and go deeper will only burn hotter.

So be practical in the evangelism efforts of your church. You are trying to reach lost people who don't care about the kind of music you sing or which version of the Bible you use. They do want to know what you have that can help change their lives. The gospel is that one thing they likely don't know they need. Share it in such a way that a child or a highly educated businessman can understand and embrace it.

I urge you to leave behind the shotgun approach and zero in on what it is God is calling you to do. When the gospel becomes the focus, lives are changed and churches grow. We must take the rifle approach and allow the gospel to be our ammunition.

CHAPTER 9

# The Compelling Gospel:
Understanding Our Responsibility with the Gospel

————⚓————

*For if I preach the gospel, I have nothing to boast of,*
*for I am under compulsion; for woe is me if I do not*
*preach the gospel.* – 1 Corinthians 9:16

It's the elephant in the room. It's the question everyone wants to ask, but very few muster the courage to ask. It invites stares in a restaurant and makes for interesting conversation starters. The question is rather simple, yet many I have met were frozen in fear of offending my wife or me. The question is this: Why would a lily-white family from Texas adopt a sweet little African girl who looks nothing like them and who had nothing in common with them?

The answer is simple. Our family adopted our precious daughter from Uganda because God laid the responsibility on our hearts to love and care for the orphans of this world. Our hearts wanted to reciprocate the love and adoption that God so graciously gave to us. We wanted to love because we were first loved.

Our adoption creates a crisis in some people's minds. "How can you be a multi-cultural family?" they wonder. "Aren't you afraid that she will grow up and know that she is different?" These types of questions cause them to be curious as to why my family would do something so radical as to love someone from a different family, culture, and continent. Questions like these often stem from false assumptions or some man-made cultural barriers. But as I mentioned, we love because we were first loved.

This is what often happens with the gospel. We allow barriers to hold us back from sharing. We back away from the life-giving message of Jesus to avoid putting ourselves or others in an uncomfortable position. We take a pass on sharing the gospel and make excuses in the process. We must come to understand our responsibility with the gospel. It's a message we cannot keep to ourselves if we truly love as we've been loved. That means becoming, as Paul wrote, all things to all men so we might by all possible means save some. It means getting outside our comfort zones, proclaiming the best news ever to people like us and people not even remotely like us. With this in mind, let me ask you a series of questions:

1. Do you believe in a literal heaven and hell?

2. Do you believe that Jesus is the only way to heaven?

3. Do you believe that anyone who does not come to faith in Jesus will be separated from God for all of eternity in hell?

If your answer was yes to these questions, and they should have been if you believe the Bible, then I have another question for you. If all of this is true, then how much must we hate someone to not share the gospel with them?

If we know that Jesus is the only way and that people will die and spend eternity in hell, shouldn't we do everything we can to lead everyone we can to faith in Jesus? Of course, the answer is yes. But in order to do this we must understand our responsibility to live and share the gospel daily in our lives. We must understand that our primary duty is not to grow our church or our career but to grow the kingdom.

Paul demonstrates this several times through the Scriptures. In the first example, Paul teaches us about a burden to preach the gospel. In 1 Corinthians 9:16, Paul says, for I am under compulsion; for woe is me if I do not preach the gospel. This attitude must permeate the hearts of pastors and churches. We cannot exist without the

> **We must understand that our primary duty is not to grow our church or our career but to grow the kingdom.**

gospel going forward. There are three main components of what Paul is communicating that the preacher must get.

First, Paul teaches us is that he is under compulsion to share the gospel. To be compelled to do something means "to drive or urge forcefully or irresistibly." He is stating that he cannot help but share the gospel. It is what drives him, gets him up in the morning, and consumes his heart and mind. His obsession is to see people come to faith in Jesus.

Is this what your life or church looks like? Do you feel the drive to win your community to faith in Christ? Paul gives us this incredible picture of a life consumed with the gospel. This is the starting point in our responsibility with the gospel, getting to the place where our heart beats to share the gospel's unending truths.

Paul teaches us that his existence is in vain if he doesn't preach the gospel. He was gifted in many things. He was a young, up-and-coming leader in his life before he met Jesus. He was poised to have power, position, and prosperity. But when Jesus changed his life, all he wanted to do was preach the gospel.

Paul was under compulsion, and nothing was more valuable than preaching Jesus to the lost. This is the mindset we must possess to fulfill the calling of the gospel. Our drive is rooted in understanding that nothing else matters in life but being the agent of the gospel in our communities. We must continually seek and pray for a heart burning to preach and live out the gospel.

Also, Paul teaches us that all of his passion to preach is not complete unless he is preaching the gospel. The gospel is the main theme of his preaching. His heart was not to preach to attract people to the temples, deliver preaching points, or gain the applause of men. His heart was that he would attract people to the King! He had at the center of his preaching one simple yet consistent theme – the gospel of Jesus.

Let's fast-forward to today's church culture. Is our preaching geared more to attract people or the presence of God? It doesn't take long when sitting in a pew to discern what the motivation behind the message is. We must remain true to the only thing that matters in our preaching and that is leading men to see the fullness of the grace of Jesus.

If not careful, we can unwittingly lose our gospel-centeredness or try to make the gospel something it's not. A few months ago my family moved to a large metropolitan area from a small town. Our first Easter in this setting was memorable. We received a heap of mailers from local churches advertising their Easter weekend services. Many of these churches advertised some great-sounding and creative sermons, yet few mentioned anything about the gospel, the cross, the resurrection, or any other gospel-

> We must shift from performance-based preaching and teaching to pleading with the lost to come to faith in Christ.

centered theme. Most of these mailers borrowed themes from popular television shows or other contemporary phenomenon to attract people. I am not railing against creativity or strategies for reaching your community, just simply stating we can and should do this with the gospel being the driving force.

The reality is that the church's primary responsibility is to communicate and exemplify the gospel. Despite what we are taught, despite worldly pressures, the church should not be concerned with the numerical growth of the local body more than it is with the kingdom. We must shift from performance-based preaching and teaching to pleading with the lost to come to faith in Christ, and reminding our members of the wonders of the gospel in every text we preach. As has been said of biblical preaching, expound on the passage and make a beeline to the cross. The "scarlet thread of redemption" runs from Genesis to Revelation. Our strategies, people, resources, and creativity must be directed to begin with the gospel and go from there.

A second example Paul gives is found in 2 Corinthians 5:17-21. In this passage, Paul shows us that it is our responsibility to share the message of Christ. He uses two phrases to show us that we are obligated to further the good news.

Notice how the phrase ministry of reconciliation clarifies that God's desire is for man's heart to be reconciled to Him. Paul deems it so significant that he tells the church at Corinth that they have the ministry of helping people become right with God. It is their obligation to help bridge the gap between man's hopelessness and God's righteousness. This burden falls to us to take the message of reconciliation to God to a hopeless world.

Another phrase Paul uses to teach us of our responsibility in the gospel is that we are ambassadors for Christ, as though God were making an appeal through us. This phrase lays out the truth that we are to speak the good news of Jesus on behalf of God. He points to us to take the initiative to be the mouthpiece for God. Our duty is to represent God in our culture. We are His ambassadors, and we must take that seriously.

The bottom line is that the gospel is our responsibility. We cannot go on ignoring the command to carry the light of the gospel into a dark world. We must love people enough to desire more than anything that they come into a relationship with Jesus. If churches will not fulfill this command, who will? If the pastor is not burdened by lost souls, how will his church see their responsibility? We must step up to embrace the gospel challenge. Our hearts must be grateful for the gospel and yet torn with the awesome responsibility of the gospel.

When I said my wedding vows to my wife, I did so because I loved her and wanted to spend the rest of my life with her. I passionately received her when her father gave her away at the front of the altar. My love for her was not the only commitment I made that day. My vows were not only to her but to her parents as well. I promised my wife that I would love, honor, and cherish her every day as long as we both shall live. I was at the same time committing to her parents that I would take good care of their daughter. I would protect her and provide for her. She not only became my wife but also my responsibility. So it is with us and the gospel. Our commitment was not only to seize the gospel for ourselves and have the promise of eternity with God, but to accept the sharing of the gospel as our responsibility also. We took on a new title, ambassador of Christ. We are to plead the gospel on His behalf.

CHAPTER 10

# Reclaiming the Lost Burden:
## Developing God's Heart for the Lost

———————◆———————

*For the Son of Man has come to seek and to save that which was lost.* – Luke 19:10

Have you ever lost something?

At about year eight of our marriage, my wife's wedding ring came up missing. We searched desperately, turning everything in our house upside down in an attempt to find it. After all, I had saved money for an entire year in college to buy it. It not only had sentimental value, but it was an expensive ring for a college-aged student to buy. We were devastated. I went to every pawnshop in our city, grasping for the hope that someone had found it and sold it. It would have been worth buying again.

This ring consumed our minds. Our phone conversations and text messages rarely concluded without asking each other if we had found the ring. There were a few nights that one of us was awakened, thinking about a new place this ring might be found. This ring really mattered, at least for a while.

After a few weeks of exhaustive searching, we began to convince ourselves that the ring was lost and would never be found. We realized we had gradually stopped looking for the ring. I wish there were a happy ending to this story – that we stumbled across it while moving from one city to another, but that just didn't happen. And so, we have given up hope of ever finding it and simply moved on. Over time, it just didn't hold as much value to us anymore.

I am afraid that this is the same place the church is today when it comes to people who are without Christ. We have lost the burden for those who are dead in their trespasses and sins. Perhaps, like my wife and me, you were once diligent and intentional about seeking out and reaching out to that which is lost, but over time the burden has quietly gone. Please allow this to be a wake-up call, a simple challenge to reclaim your burden for the lost.

The evident heartbeat of Jesus was to seek out the lost and dying. He makes a revolutionary statement in Luke 19:10 when He says, For the Son of Man has come to seek and to save that which was lost. Jesus clearly communicates His passion and mission statement here. He knew the glories of heaven and the horrors of hell. He knew firsthand what those who died without placing faith in Him would miss out on. He was driven by the burden. If Jesus had this burden for the lost, how much more should we?

> **We make every excuse possible for why our churches are not seeing people come to faith in Christ.**

One of the major issues in churches today is apathy for those who are living in darkness. We make every excuse possible for why our churches are not seeing people come to faith in Christ.

But no one wants to deal with the real issue, that we have let other things become more important than the lost.

As the director of evangelism in a Baptist ministry, I am privileged to be around pastors. I travel my state and meet with pastors to talk about evangelism. In one particular meeting, a pastor spoke transparently. He told our small group meeting that his church hadn't been burdened for the lost. He said that as the pastor, he had not been burdened, but was signifying his commitment to change. We need more pastors like him. The reality is that most churches will follow the heart of a pastor who is burdened for the lost and will reflect his agenda.

The Bible gives us a great example of living with a burden for the gospel. This story in Mark 2 describes a helpless and hopeless paralytic whose entire life had been marked by disability. He had no chance for a future apart from a miracle. He was paralyzed both physically and spiritually. However, one thing distinguished him from every other paralytic that day: He had friends who were burdened.

As this story unfolds, Jesus was preaching in a house to a standing-room-only crowd. The people in this room were not only hearing the Word being preached to them by its Author, they were about to become a part of history as Jesus healed a man spiritually and physically. And all because four men were burdened for their friend. Notice three things in the passage about their burden that led to his life change.

## THEIR BURDEN REQUIRED ACTION

It is one thing to have a deep-rooted burden for someone you know is lost; it's another to do something about it. Most people would admit the most difficult people to share their faith with are those who are closest to them. These four men could have ignored their heart's cry for this man. They could have had previous engagements that they were unwilling to reschedule. But that is not the picture we see here. We see four men so burdened for their friend that they were going to stop at nothing to get him before Jesus.

Where is this resolve found in your church today? We have programs galore for the various life stages of our church members. Our children's programs and youth events will be fully staffed with volunteers, yet if we plan to leave the church property to verbally share Jesus, a handful show up. We tend toward contentment rather than carrying a burden for the lost that should weigh heavily on our hearts.

I have seen people literally lose sleep over something discussed in a church business meeting. But in many cases, these people have never lost a wink of sleep over someone's eternal destiny. They have never been consumed with the thought that a friend or relative could spend eternity in hell, apart from God. This is a direct result of our churches losing the burden for lost souls.

These four men are great examples of burden being validated by action. They wanted to see their friend healed in more than one way. They took the initiative to pick him up and bring him to Jesus. Once we become burdened, we must act upon that burden. We must move from the emotional realm into the physical realm.

## THEIR BURDEN REQUIRED DETERMINATION

These four men are heroes whom we should tell our children and grandchildren to model themselves after. They not only had a deep-rooted burden for their friend, they acted upon the burden. The interesting thing is that they had no idea what obstacles they would face.

Want to know if someone has a burden for something? See what he or she is willing to go through to lift that burden. When people will walk through difficulty and barriers and continue on the journey, you know they feel called by God to the task. These four men were a great example of focus and perseverance motivated by their burden.

The paralytic was blessed to have friends who were burdened for him. They had to overcome several barriers to get him to Jesus. But Jesus blessed their efforts.

One has to wonder what would have happened in our culture today if this were our church members. Would they have given up once they saw the size of the crowd? Would they have apologized to their friend and returned him to his pallet to waste his life away? Would they have been willing to destroy a man's roof to accomplish their mission? Would they have been willing to just say that they tried their best? Of course, we do not know these answers. But we do have people today who will not come to church if they must sit too close to someone or who get mad and leave over personal preferences. We could go on for pages about trivial reasons why people will not get involved in church or why they leave their church. The point is this: When you're burdened for spiritually dead people, all that matters is to succeed in the mission. When you're not burdened, you make every excuse to dismiss yourself from the responsibility.

## THEIR BURDEN REQUIRED FAITH

A third step to their friend's transformation was their faith. They believed enough in what Jesus could do for this man that they were willing to do whatever it took to get him there. Their belief was that if they did their part in getting their friend there, Jesus would bless their efforts.

One of the reasons we are not burdened is we seem to forget what Jesus can do. I have never met a man that Jesus could not and was not willing to change. There is no person so far gone that Jesus can't transform him. We must believe it and act on it.

These men put feet to their faith. They went through the necessary struggles to see their friend be made new inside and out. This same faith can still be attained today. We must believe that Jesus can save anyone. We must act upon it with the people we know are not in a relationship with Jesus.

> **I have never met a man that Jesus could not and was not willing to change.**

When you lose the burden for the unregenerate, you have lost the heart of Jesus. There is a danger of this happening subtly, almost without our noticing. We sing our songs, go to our Sunday school classes, and hear our preacher, but then forget we have been commissioned by Jesus to reach the world. This must change if we are to see an awakening.

We must come back to the heart of Jesus to seek out the lost. Francis Chan says this well in the foreword to David Platt's book Follow Me. He says, "I see a trend in many churches where people are beginning to enjoy convicting sermons. They walk out feeling broken over their sin. The distorted part is that they can begin to feel victorious in their sadness ... The focus is on the conviction itself and not the change it is meant to produce."[3] So how does this happen practically?

First, we must teach our responsibility with the gospel. As I stated in chapter 9, we must get people to a place of understanding the call, for every believer is to share the good news of Jesus. It is up to us; we are His ambassadors.

Second, we must teach our people to be aware of those around them. We live in a fast-paced society. We must teach them to always be aware of when they may need to slow down and share the gospel. We see this awareness in these four men written about in Mark 2. We also see it in many cases with Jesus throughout His ministry.

Third, we need to equip the people to be all in until the mission is accomplished. I will talk more about equipping in another chapter. However, we must realize that when we surrendered to Jesus, it was forever. An interesting development in our culture today is the prenuptial agreement. People plan how things will be sorted out in case their marriage doesn't make it. In other words, the vows and commitments they make at the altar come with a "Plan B." This seems ironic to speak of prenuptials, vows, and commitments in the same sentence. Yet this same mindset is now in the church. People join a church and stay until they don't like something, and then they bail to the next church. The sad thing is we sometimes mistake this church hopping as church growth. We need to lead people to be all in as disciples and members of the covenant community.

I wonder what our nation would look like today if we were truly burdened for the masses of unconverted people. I can only imagine what the churches would be able to accomplish in taking care of the widows and orphans, feeding the hungry, clothing the naked, and helping the homeless if we were passionately burdened. May the Lord burden you and me to our deepest core for the lost.

# CHAPTER 11

# Motivating and Mobilizing:

## Getting People Excited About
## the Great Commission

—◆—

*Follow Me and I will make you become fishers
of men.* – Mark 1:17

S ome of the greatest events in America's history have come
on the heels of moments or speeches that motivated people to action. Dr. Martin Luther King Jr.'s famous "I Have a
Dream" speech catapulted the civil rights movement. President George W. Bush's speech at Ground Zero following the
9/11 attacks set the course
for our nation's resolve in
the War on Terror. Many
great halftime speeches have
given athletes the necessary
burst of energy and effort to
come from behind and win
the game. These speeches turned gloom into motivation and
inspired people to take action and experience victory.

> **Motivation is a seed that
> buries itself in the depths of
> the human heart, and when
> the time is right causes a
> harvest of heroic action.**

Motivation is a seed that buries itself in the depths of the
human heart, and when the time is right causes a harvest of

heroic action. It can inspire someone to do something far greater than they could have ever imagined. It has at its core the power to change a situation instantaneously. Motivation is the key that unlocks the door of productivity and success.

In a culture that has fallen ill with the disease of apathy, motivation can help turn the tide and position us for success. The church needs it to once again stand strong and move forward with the mission set forth to us by Jesus Himself. Believers across the world need to be motivated and mobilized to fulfill the Great Commission. The time to do this is now.

We have never experienced a more fertile ground to plant the seeds of the gospel than we have now. We have more people walking on the planet than ever. We also have the great benefits of technology to assist us in the efforts of spreading the gospel. Yet we are not seeing the gospel sweeping the planet like we know it has the power to do.

Why is this? Have we lost our motivation and desire to be the agent of the gospel? Have we lost our burden for people who don't have a relationship with the Lord? Have we forgotten the urgency of the gospel? I say the answer is a resounding yes to all of these. We simply are not motivated to see people come to Christ and be incorporated into the church body.

This trend must change. We are in desperate need of motivated people who are mobilized with the gospel. This must take place in the local church. The church is the vehicle that will drive the gospel forward. The church is the catalyst that must spring people into action.

We know the gospel has the power to change lives now and for all of eternity. We know that the Great Commission commands us to take the gospel to the ends of the earth. We know that people who do not come to faith in Jesus Christ will spend eternity in hell. Therefore, we must learn to motivate people to take the responsibility of the gospel seriously. This truth lends itself to a major question: How do we motivate and mobilize people to be agents of the gospel?

I can think of at least three great motivators we see in the Bible. Their lives can teach us how to get our people excited about telling the good news of Jesus. They can point us in the right direction to maximize our effectiveness with the gospel.

## PETER

Peter was a great motivator. He was usually the first to step up and be heard. He experienced many great times with Jesus because He was unafraid to take risks. Once such time was when Jesus was asking His disciples who people thought He was. The other disciples injected the opinions of others while Peter was quick to answer the Lord's question of who do you say that I am? Peter's response and understanding invited praise from Jesus and an anointing of leadership for the church (Matthew 16:13-20). Even though he was a great leader, Peter also made mistakes. These mistakes would knock him down, but not out. He learned and led through his mistakes and would become one of the most influential men in history.

You could say Peter was the main leader of the twelve disciples. He was usually the point man in a story, being the vocal one of the group. He was the leader because he rose to the occasion when it was necessary, and sometimes when it wasn't.

Leadership doesn't go around looking for conflict; conflict looks for leaders. This made Peter valuable to Jesus. In the moments that would count, Peter would be there. Though not always in the positive light, Peter would always be involved.

I can't tell you how many times I have heard people criticize Peter for falling in the water as he took his eyes off Jesus. But because he was a leader, he is only the second man in history to know what it feels like to walk on the waves. I have heard people criticize him for cutting off the ear of the soldier in the garden. Yet how many of the other disciples stood up and fought for their Savior? Peter was a leader who knew how to get in the mix and bring people along with him.

> **Leadership doesn't go around looking for conflict; conflict looks for leaders.**

Peter used words to motivate. Though he failed Jesus in the crucial hours leading up to the crucifixion, Peter was restored and knew he had a purpose to live out. He would go on to deliver the sermon that changed the world as we know it. His words at Pentecost sparked a movement unlike what the world had ever seen. In just a few words, God used Peter to motivate thousands of people to leave the religion of their fathers and grandfathers and to follow Jesus as Messiah.

Peter's words would echo across the world and help launch the organized church as we know it. The reason we have a portrait of a vibrant, healthy church in Acts 2 was his ability to preach the gospel along with the Spirit and to motivate people to follow Christ. We can enjoy Christianity in America, in part, due to Peter's motivation of those believers in the days following the death of Christ. It was the seedbed for evangelization of the known world.

Our words are a great source of motivation. We have the ability as pastors and leaders to say things that will spur people on to greatness. Our words can be the fuel that burns the fire of the gospel in someone's heart. Most of us were saved through hearing the gospel being proclaimed by someone who motivated us to see our sinfulness and our great need for a Savior. This is the power of what we say.

One word of caution when talking about motivating people to be agents of the gospel: Remember, words can discourage just as they encourage. I know of pastors who beat people down with their words if they don't see them sharing the gospel. We must remember that we are to equip the saints, not abuse them. Our responsibility as leaders is to motivate them to the gospel, not cause them to resent the work. We must choose our words carefully while understanding that we have a great tool to motivate people to look more like Jesus.

## PAUL

Paul was a great leader who was also used by God to motivate people to do radical things for the gospel. His undeniable call to be the mouthpiece of the gospel and to initiate missions is unparalleled today. His courage and tenacity gives us a standard by which we should strive to live. We know that Paul loved to preach and teach. We know that Paul had an unusual ability to network people together. His mentoring of young Timothy has been a consistent challenge to the church of mentorship and discipleship for many centuries. However, history would prove to us that Paul's greatest ability to motivate people came through his writing. Paul wrote a large portion of the New Testament. You might call Paul the world's first best-selling author.

It is noteworthy that before Paul's conversion, we don't hear anything about his writing ability. We know that he was a leader in attacking the church at the pleasure of the high priest. Yet the same man who was at the root of the great persecution of the church in Jerusalem would one day motivate millions on their journey to faith in Jesus.

Paul had a following. Ministers wanted to be around him. He was influential all the way around. He used his influence against the church before converting to Christianity. After his experience with Jesus, he used his influence to change the course of history, becoming a missionary and church planter. Of all his accolades and accomplishments, writing became his greatest asset.

Paul teaches us that we can motivate people outside of conventional methods like speaking or preaching. Many authors echo Paul's mode of motivation. Most people have read a great book in their lifetime that caused them to take some type of action. Bookshelves are lined with physical fitness books to spur people to healthy habits. There are books on marriage to help a couple become motivated to pursue a great marriage. There are books on finances to help people become wealthy. All of these are great examples of the power of written words.

One of the greatest things we can do as ministers is to use our writing ability to move people. Notes of encouragement in a dark season leave deep impressions, sometimes decades later. We can write notes of congratulations to those who begin new pursuits. We can write notes of thanks to those who have helped us accomplish something. The point is that God gives us the ability to motivate through writing; we should use it.

## STEPHEN

Stephen's story in the Bible is one of the most impactful short stories we read. Stephen was a promising leader in the Christian faith. He is characterized in Acts as full of faith and of the Holy Spirit (Acts 6:5). While his life is briefly described, his influence is still greatly felt. The power of his motivation is in his example.

God was using Stephen in a great way when the trouble started for him. He was speaking truth powerfully and that displeased some men. They began spreading lies and brought him before the high priest. Stephen gave his defense and was martyred for his faith. In his death he motivated people to experience life.

Stephen's message caused anger and bitterness from the people, such that they put him out of the city and began stoning him to death. While the stones and insults were flying, Stephen, full of the Holy Spirit, was praying and asking God to forgive those who were executing him. His motivation came from his willingness to die for his Savior.

Upon his final breath, a great persecution began to rise against the church. It was so intense that the people had to scatter. They went their separate ways and were faced with the challenge of spreading the message amid persecution. But Stephen's commitment to Christ was fresh in their memory and fueled their desire to take the gospel to new places. They were willing to go because he was willing to die. His example spurred them on in obedience to Christ.

They could have given up, retreated, and stopped sharing about Jesus. But their friend stood firm until the end. This gave them motivation to become mobile agents of the gospel.

As pastors and leaders, we must motivate by exemplifying what it looks like to live out the gospel daily. Our flocks watch us to see if we practice what we preach. It needs to be evident that we as leaders are walking daily with our Lord through His Word, consistency in prayer, practicing faith in what God can do, and intentionally sharing our faith. Our people will be more likely to follow our example if they know that we are living out these truths ourselves.

> **The way in which we live will motivate our church to be agents of the gospel or discourage them from being all in.**

Paul shows us what this looks like in 1 Thessalonians chapter 1 as he tells the church that the gospel was not given to them in word, but that they led by example for them as well. Their leading by example motivated the people in Thessalonica to imitate their walk and therefore lives were changed. This goes to show us that the way in which we live will motivate our church to be agents of the gospel or discourage them from being all in.

We must take this seriously. Your church will follow you as long as you believe and help them to believe in the cause you are excited about.

I remember a season of great growth in a church that I pastored. We saw God do some amazing things and had to address space issues. We met for months trying to develop a plan that would empower us to better reach our community. We came up with a plan that seemed great at the time but now sounds a little crazy: we met in a tent in the parking lot for six weeks, as we remodeled our sanctuary to make room for the growth we were experiencing. I know by itself that doesn't sound too radical, but those six weeks were in December and January. Texas isn't North Dakota, but it gets cold in Texas too.

I will never forget those early Sunday mornings getting to the church around daylight to start the commercial-size heaters in the tent. It was a great six weeks that will forever be treasured for me and for the church. Even though this was an unconventional move for us, the people were willing to do anything because they were excited. This move motivated them to become mobile in talking about what God was doing at our church. This goes to prove that if we get people passionate, excited, and motivated for the lost, there are really no limits to what they can do for the kingdom.

# CHAPTER 12

# Developing the Strategy:

## Aim at Nothing, Hit It Every Time

————————•┴•————————

*For which one of you, when he wants to build a
tower, does not first sit down and calculate the cost
to see if he has enough to complete it?* – Luke 14:28

When I was younger, one of the things I enjoyed doing
the most was putting something together. Having hundreds of parts scattered out everywhere excited me because I
knew could assemble them and make something great. I would
spend hours upon hours putting an object together piece by
piece. This exercise engaged my young mind because I always
was thinking one step ahead. I was in the assembly process.
I had a picture in my mind of what this object was going to
look like. Therefore, the process was not mundane or labor
intensive; it was an exciting time of seeing a magnificent and
useful product being built to last. As leaders in the church, this
can be our mindset when we dream and work on our strategy.
When we believe big for the future, the process of development
and implementation isn't something to dread, but to embrace.

I am a visionary! I love to dream big dreams and watch them
come true. This is one of the greatest joys of ministry. I have

taken the approach that God has something big He wants to do in and through us. He knows our abilities and limitations. I teach that God did not call us to mediocrity, but to excellence. This belief system should drive our dreaming and vision to reach the world for Christ. We must have a big vision from God, but we must also develop a practical strategy to carry out this vision. This chapter will help begin the process of developing a practical strategy for your church.

Creating an evangelism strategy in the local church is a contextual matter. What will work in metro areas may not be as successful in rural America. But there are some common aspects of evangelism strategies that apply in all contexts. Therefore, each evangelism strategy should be unique to the church and its community. In order to assist you as you think through your unique context, let's begin by asking a few diagnostic questions:

1. What is the demographic makeup of your community?

2. What has been done in evangelism at your church in the past that was successful?

3. What will the people in your church be willing to do to reach the community?

4. Are you, as the leader, willing to risk it all for this vision?

5. What can you identify today that is holding you back from developing a great evangelism strategy for your church?

An evangelism strategy must extend from the vision of the pastor's or church leader's heart. As Ed Stetzer puts it, "It must come from the pastor because God has uniquely anointed the pastor to present His vision to the congregation."[4] The vision must find its origin in three things. First, it must come from the biblical mandate found in Acts 1:8. Many churches focus on a global missions strategy. This is doable through mission trips and continuing partnerships around the world. Unfortunately, for many churches the global initiative overshadows the need for local evangelism and missions. Acts 1:8 shows that the church must be multi-tiered in its evangelism. Participation in global evangelism is necessary, but churches must reach their Jerusalem … Judea and Samaria, and even to the remotest part of the earth (Acts 1:8). Churches must have a focus in their own backyards. The mission begins in your "Jerusalem."

The second place from which the vision must come is a genuine heart for the unsaved. Believers must understand God's heart when the Bible says the Lord is not wishing for any to perish but for all to come to repentance (2 Peter 3:9). This heartbeat will propel the church to fulfill the Great Commission. A pastor must lead by example if his people are to follow. If a pastor does not have a heart and a burden for the lost, neither will the people he leads.

The third place from which the vision must come is the successful example of others. When a pastor sees a legitimate model of successful evangelism, it should spur him to envision how evangelism could be done successfully in his context. As Rick Warren says, "anytime I see a program working in another church, I try to extract the principle behind it and apply it in our church."[5] This can be done through research and church visitation where God has moved through a biblically sound strategy.

Envisioning and developing an evangelism strategy in the local church will only happen if the pastor or leader is all

> **Envisioning and developing an evangelism strategy in the local church will only happen if the pastor or leader is all in for the vision.**

in for the vision. A workable strategy takes much organization and support from leaders and volunteers, which makes it imperative that the lead person is fully supportive and will use his platform to promote it. When pastor-leaders are leading out, evangelism strategies tend to flourish.

I can identify at least five areas that are crucial for a church-wide evangelism emphasis to succeed. It is important these areas be handled diligently and bathed in prayer, for they will develop the process the strategy must follow. These five areas are:

## ADVANCE PLANNING

A church cannot develop an excellent evangelism strategy without planning far in advance. Without it, the people the church befriends will not be adequately accommodated nor will a great first impression be given. The adage "a failure to plan is a plan to fail" holds true. But "effective planners know the time they take to plan will ultimately pay dividends."[6]

Obviously, when a church is dealing with people's souls, diligence matters. This will afford the most opportunities for a lost person to come to a place of saving faith. So take all the time needed to execute the strategy with excellence. No mediocrity allowed.

The advance-planning checklist goes like this: First, it is wise for a church to plan all aspects of their strategy one year out. This will allow the church to check with all city, school, and community calendars to avoid conflicting events and allow cooperation amongst all parties, so they can work hand in hand on ensuring the strategy will be a success.

A second suggestion is to involve sympathetic community leaders and businesses in the strategy. Though the effort is church ministry, many businesses often wish to contribute to things that will benefit the community. This benefits the church's relationships and may ease budgeting costs. This sends a great message to the community that churches and businesses are working together to strengthen the community. The solicitation of business involvement will need to take place six months prior to any event that you may host. It is a good idea for one to meet directly with the manager of a business to explain all facets of the event.

Third, it is imperative to have an adequate number of volunteers. Having enough volunteers will allow the leader to be freed up from details in order to lead. As Leith Anderson writes, "most of the work of the local church is done by volunteers. If the volunteers are ministering effectively, the church is ministering effectively."[7] The enlisting of volunteers must be an ongoing effort.

Advance planning for a strategy is a must. A well-executed strategy that will utilize ample volunteers and draw lost people requires hours of discussion, planning, and resourcing.

## TARGETED AUDIENCE AND EVENT

A second area of focus in a strategy is the narrowing of the audience you are trying to reach. This should be a simple task, but it can easily become very difficult. An old proverb teaches that if you aim at nothing, you will hit it every time. This is true in church planning and strategy as well. Therefore, the church must decide on two factors with everything they do: Who is their "Jerusalem" and what type of approach should they take in reaching it?

First, in the advance-planning stage, a church must determine its targeted audience for particular parts of the strategy. This decision will in turn determine the entire strategy. For example, if a church is trying to reach young families, it will want to focus its efforts on things relating to children. This will be more attractive to parents thinking of attending a church. But bounce-houses and cotton candy aren't as useful in a neighborhood of retirees. A church must attend to its targeted audience to effectively carry out the strategy.

> **An old proverb teaches that if you aim at nothing, you will hit it every time.**

To know who that audience is, churches must determine the demographics of the area. There are many ways this can be done. For example, one author suggests that the church "gain insight as to the demographics you are considering by using the Internet, library, city hall, chamber of commerce, etc."[8] This will give a clear picture of who is in the area where the church hopes to evangelize.

Another assessment involves the spiritual state of the area where the effort will focus. Asking this question will allow churches to identify the most unchurched areas. Then, the church must ask how they can relate to those people. From this, the church can enlist the volunteers who would be most effective in serving that area.

Once a church answers these questions, it can then determine what type of approach would be most effective for its purposes. Not only must the planning identify the targeted audience, but it must also develop a strategy to reach that audience. The strategy will be created to draw people, but it must be the right approach. For example, if a church wants to reach singles, then it would be more effective if the singles in the church are the leading participants and the outreach takes place where singles are found.

**BUDGET ALLOCATION**

A third area of focus must be budget allocation, another crucial aspect. A strategy must be funded in order to have all the necessary ingredients for excellence. As McNamara and Davis say, "It costs to reach your community, but money spent on evangelism is never an expense, it's always an investment."[9] For this to happen, the leader must be diligent in his preparation. Churches will find that evangelism can be done on a tight budget if carefully planned. At a church I pastored, block parties were a common outreach. Over the years the church has figured out a formula that works for around two thousand dollars per block party. This is an effective, relatively low-cost strategy for the church family that can produce many transformed lives if gospel-focused.

When planning a strategy, the leaders must make a list of everything needed to execute the plan. For example, serving food requires paper goods, condiments, and drinks to go with it. The church also needs to list all costs associated with entertainment. (This could include inflatables, music, giveaways, and all other costs.) These lists will help a church accurately budget for the block party and allow it to track the actual cost of the event.

A leader needs to know one additional thing about budget allocation for his church's evangelism strategy. If he does not budget for the strategy, it is most likely sunk. Churches must be intentional in putting these types of service events into the budget. In his book Total Church Life, Darrell Robinson says, "Every church and organizational leader should be equipped for intentional witnessing.... The church should budget at least a tithe, 10 percent, to evangelism events and activities."[10] If a church does not budget money for intentional evangelism, something else will use up the funds. When a church is serious about evangelism, it will be serious about funding it.

> **If a church does not budget money for intentional evangelism, something else will use up the funds.**

## SPECIFIC GOAL SETTING

A fourth important area of focus in developing an evangelism strategy in the local church is specific goal setting. As Bracken, Timmreck, and Church suggest, "goal setting is the first step in the developmental planning process. A key principle in goal setting is that participation in setting the goal produces the commitment and motivation to pursue it."[11] Churches that set goals will be less likely to quit until they have reached the goal for which they are striving. In the pursuit of winning people to Jesus, churches should set two categories of goals. First, churches need to focus on the goals that are reachable with rightly allocated resources and a sufficient staff.

These goals must be attainable and have an appropriate target audience. For example, a church in a town of three thousand people could host a community block party and set a goal of seeing two hundred people show up at the event. From that numerical goal, the church could also pray for at least five people to give their lives to Jesus.

> **Churches should set attainable goals, but leave room for God to do the unimaginable. He is more than able.**

With the right resources and people serving, and with the gospel being preached to two hundred unchurched people, that prayer could conceivably be realized. Moreover, reaching a goal will provide a boost of excitement for the church and will allow it to see that when it sets a goal and works hard, the goal can be reached, and souls won for eternity.

Secondly, the above said, churches should also set goals that are beyond what they could accomplish on their own efforts; that is, churches need goals that can only be accomplished if God intervenes. Many churches only set goals that are easily attainable. But churches should have a hope and an expectation for God to work exceedingly beyond anything they could dream of. Remember, unless God is in the process, everything we do is in vain. Our goals should invite the Holy Spirit to do what only He can do. Churches should set attainable goals, but leave room for God to do the unimaginable. He is more than able.

When setting goals for evangelism, a leadership team should focus on three priorities, the first being the number of unchurched people who will be embraced. A church must remember: The driving motivation is to see unconverted people come to faith in Jesus. Setting this type of numerical goal of touching a certain number will help determine where and how to reach these people with the gospel of Jesus Christ.

This can be done in numerous ways. You can serve free food, have giveaways, or offer activities that are geared for the group you're trying to reach, such as water slides for families with young children. Ultimately, however, unchurched people come to events when the church is proactively investing and inviting them to attend.

A second priority for a strategy needs to be how many people the church expects will receive Jesus as their Lord and Savior. Call it a dream sheet if you will, realizing too that God can do above and beyond our dreams. Darrel Vaughan says it simply: "[W]hen we pray for a revival, we can expect God to move."[12] This principle applies to any aspect of an evangelism strategy. We must expect a movement from God. This is why we do evangelism. Church leaders should be realistic and yet have faith that God will do more than they could ever expect. Nevertheless, setting a numerical "dream sheet" for how many could accept Christ allows the volunteers to have something tangible for which to pray.

A third priority for churches is a timeline goal for follow-up. This is especially important at events. As Allison and Anderson urge, "for local churches that want to host regular evangelistic events, make sure the follow-up leaders are ready."[13] Churches must stand ready and able to follow up. For example, if a person comes to faith in Christ at an event, the church needs to follow up with the person and explain the process of baptism to him or her in a timely manner. Follow-up is as important as any other part of the event.

## INCORPORATION INTO THE CHURCH

The final area that needs attention when developing and implementing an evangelism strategy is how best to help incorporate people into the church body. Proper follow-up after an event will help people assimilate into the local body and lays a foundation for their future church relationships. When one comes to faith in Christ, he or she needs to become introduced to the covenant community as soon as possible. As Searcy and Henson state, "you want to have a clear, simple way of getting people plugged into the next step."[14] Many people seem to fall off the wagon after making the life-changing decision to follow Jesus. This is often because they did not know what step to take next. Therefore, this is an essential part of the advance planning stages of the strategy. We'll talk more on this in a later chapter.

There must be a vision but also a practical plan to carry out the vision. It's one thing for a pastor to speak about what God wants the church to do and another to give the church the road map of how to get there. The majority of people who fill the seats in a church need and desire specific action plans. The leadership has the responsibility to give this direction to them.

# CHAPTER 13

# Keys to Implementing Your Strategy:

## Communicating for Change

———— ◆ ————

*And on the Sabbath day we went outside the gate to a
riverside, where we were supposing that there would be
a place of prayer; and we sat down and began speaking
to the women who had assembled. – Acts 16:13*

I am a runner. I love to put on my shoes and hit the road for
a few miles almost daily. There is nothing quite like being
out on a long stretch of the road alone, music in your ears,
pushing yourself to go just one more mile. Running becomes
an addiction. What starts out to be something one might do
for exercise can become a beast that must continuously be fed.

The first day that I started running, I was so out of shape
that I had to stop three times in the first quarter-mile. I felt like
I would never accomplish any kind of real distance. But each
day I went out and pushed myself to go a little farther than I
did the day before.

Only a few months into my running, I decided to train for
a marathon. I wanted to be a part of the elite group who chal-

lenge their bodies to run for 26.2 miles without stopping. The goal of finishing a marathon seemed daunting and impossible. I wasn't quite sure that I could do it. That's when I figured out there was more to running than just putting on shoes and getting out the door.

The thing that I came to realize through my friend Boog Ferrell (a coach who has mastered countless endurance runs) was that planning your run was crucial. You need to chart a course to run and make sure that along the route, you set out water or small snacks to keep yourself hydrated and energized.

Planning your run is significant, but implementing the plan is the key to success. You could plan a twelve-mile route down to the finest detail, but if you don't physically place the water and snacks along the way (implementation), you will be in danger of getting dehydrated and too weak to finish.

As churches, we must not only plan, we must also take action to implement the plan. This is not always easy, yet always necessary. A vision without action is deemed useless and will end in frustration for your church. Paul gives us a great example of this in Acts 16 when God calls him to go to Macedonia. Acts 16:10-13 says:

> **A vision without action is deemed useless and will end in frustration for your church.**

When he had seen the vision, immediately we sought to go into Macedonia, concluding that God had called us to preach the gospel to them. So putting out to sea from Troas, we ran a straight course to Samothrace, and on the day following to Neapolis; and from there to Philippi, which is a leading city of the district of Macedonia, a Roman colony; and we were staying in this city for some days. And on the Sabbath day we went outside the gate to a riverside, where we were supposing that there would be a place of prayer; and we sat down and began speaking to the women who had assembled.

Paul knew God wanted him to go and share the gospel. Even more than that, Paul knew that he wasn't to just sit around waiting on someone to come to him. He intentionally went down to the river to tell the women about Jesus. It's not enough to know there's a plan. We have to implement the plan God has given us.

Once a pastor or church leader has developed the strategy for evangelism, work must begin on its implementation. This can be a challenging yet rewarding time for the pastor and his ministry. Below are four actions I have outlined to help you implement an effective evangelism strategy for your church.

## COMMUNICATE THE STRATEGY WITH GREAT PASSION

First, it is vitally important for a pastor to communicate the goals of the strategy to his congregation. This is a key aspect of making the strategy successful. People want a clear vision to follow that shows them how they can make a difference. Therefore, the pastor must cast the vision with excellence or it will fail. As Malphurs teaches, "If the pastor struggles as a vision caster, the church may be in trouble."[15] Therefore, a pastor must have an internal conviction regarding the vision. This is important because a clearly communicated vision can light a flame in the church. This can be done by a pastor or leader, showing the people the foundation and goals of the strategy.

In turn, it should point people to the heart of the Great Commission and the purpose of the church.

When communicating such a strategy to the church, avoid mundane details. In the most concise and simplest way possible, share the vision to reach people and explain how the church will accomplish that goal. That said, the pastor must let the people play an integral role in how the model comes together.

A second guideline for a pastor to consider when communicating the vision is the scriptural mandate for serving and evangelizing. As Ryan Doeller puts it, "The Great Commission is a biblical mandate which should be considered by all believers as an obligatory part of their faith."[16] Scripture is the pastor's greatest foundation upon which to build. If a pastor points his people to the demands in Scripture for believers to love by serving and sharing the gospel, then reaching people for Jesus is the obedient next step for the church.

> **If a pastor points his people to the demands in Scripture for believers to love by serving and sharing the gospel, then reaching people for Jesus is the obedient next step for the church.**

A third guideline for communicating the vision is showing the church the extent of lostness surrounding them. This can be done by presenting demographics research. If people see the number of lost people nearby, they will be more likely to get involved in reaching them. When a pastor communicates with accurate statistics, it further validates his plea for the church to enter into a strategy to change the statistics for the better. A great resource for these statistics can be found at the website of the North American Mission Board.[17]

**SELL THE STRATEGY TO KEY LEADERS WITHIN THE CHURCH**

If a pastor wants to gain the church's approval for a strategy, he will first need to win over the key leaders in the church. This will give him the vocal support of respected people. Pastors come and go, but people of influence in a church, be they good, bad, or a little of both, are often there to stay. So if a pastor can gain the support of the key leaders, he will set the strategy up for success. The pastor needs to meet often with the leaders to repeatedly communicate the vision. As Webster states, "Senior pastors will need to conduct several meetings throughout the week with their key leaders." [18] While the number of meetings will vary, the important point is that pastors strive to meet with these leaders.

At this point, it is helpful to distinguish a "key leader" from other church members. The following criteria can be useful as guidelines: A key leader is one who will fulfill four requirements. First, he is someone who tithes biblically to the church. Second, the leader must have some tenure at the church. A key leader will have been at the church long enough to know the heritage of the church. Third, a key leader must have integrity cultivated from sincerely following Christ. Having a reputation as a person of integrity is something that must be earned. Last, a key leader should be classified as one who actively serves in the church. This is important because a leader cannot lead without also serving. If the pastor takes adequate time to share the vision with the key leaders of the church, he will find that the road to implementing the new strategy can be quite smooth.

## BE DIRECTLY INVOLVED IN THE STRATEGY

A pastor will often allow people to start ministries in the church while avoiding involvement himself. However, Patrick Morley's research shows that:

"[The] most striking finding was the level of personal involvement by the successful senior pastor. This is not to say that the senior pastor has to do everything. In the successful churches other pastors or laymen often did the work – but the senior pastor never fully let go."[19]

For an evangelism strategy to be executed with success, the pastor must not only share the vision, but lead by example in the vision. This is not to say that the pastor should be dictatorial; he merely needs to be a part of the strategy in action.

Pastors would do well to appoint a team to be in charge of specific aspects of the vision, and the pastor must pledge his wholehearted support by being vocal and present throughout the strategy. People follow the pastor's example; they will be a part of what the pastor is a part of. The pastor should be on the frontlines, serving and sharing Christ at these events.

## KEEP THE STRATEGY IN FRONT OF THE CONGREGATION

Today's culture will abandon something if it believes there is a better option. If the pastor is not keeping this strategy in the consciousness of the people, they will be distracted by some other need, causing their heart for evangelism to diminish.

In order for a pastor to keep this type of strategy in the people's minds, the vision must be refreshed continuously. Many times churches will execute several events with excellence, but have no clear vision for implementing the strategy in the future. The strategy must be deeply embedded in the pastor's heart, making it natural for him to keep it on the people's minds.

One way to keep the strategy fresh on people's minds is to talk about and celebrate the successes. People like to see results, and if they are told of the number of people coming to faith in the Lord, they will continue to get excited and will most likely stay involved.

Implementing an evangelism strategy in the church is not a difficult task. When God places a burden in the heart of a church to reach the lost, the church will see results. As Dodd says, "When we get God's burden, it will be aligned with His passionate focus on the least, the last, and the lost."[20] Churches

> **When God places a burden in the heart of a church to reach the lost, the church will see results.**

must spend time asking God to use them to change the surrounding culture. It is one thing to talk about the need to reach people, but another to implement a strategy and see God move.

I challenge you today not only to have a plan detailed for your people but also a tangible call to action. People are ready to carry out the plan as long as the leader owns it and helps implement it. God has blessed you with a people who are not to sit still but to go and act upon the vision He gives to you!

# CHAPTER 14

# The Faith Test:

## Expecting God to Do What Only He Can Do

———— ⚓ ————

*Son of man, can these bones live?* – Ezekiel 37:3

I t started out as an ordinary day. My wife and I arose from bed to head off to the doctor's office for an ultrasound. It was our second child. I will never forget sitting in the waiting room with butterflies in my stomach. My heart seemed to beat a thousand times faster each time the door opened and the nurse appeared to call out the next patient's name. Time seemed to linger as our excitement built. After what felt like an eternity, they called our name.

We made our way to the back room where the ultrasound machines were. It was a nice-sized room that had held many families as they viewed their babies. As the technician began the ultrasound, we watched every move on the machine and were amazed at how technology allowed us to meet this child before the due date. This was shaping up to be a great day. It all changed with five brief words: "Excuse me for a moment."

She exited the room to get the doctor. My wife and I locked eyes, knowing this happy moment was presenting something that would affect our lives forever. I knew that whatever was happening, I needed to be strong and encouraging for my wife. I whispered to her, "Whatever is happening, we will walk in faith." These words would prove to be more difficult than I thought, even as God was faithful to sustain us.

The doctor told us the devastating news: somehow, our child did not make it, and we would have to schedule the delivery of a stillborn little boy whom we named Konner. One of the most difficult realities of my life was to wheel my wife into the hospital to have a baby, only to wheel her out without a baby in her arms.

In the moments following the delivery, I walked toward the waiting room to get the family to come and comfort my wife. As I was making my way down the hallway, I found a little area where there were no patients. I hit the floor and cried out to God, asking questions about why He did this and why He did this to us. I didn't understand it. I had surrendered my life to Him. I had made the commitment to serve Him full time in ministry. I was a pastor, and we were faithfully walking with Him.

It didn't seem right and certainly not fair. There at the end of the hallway, I laid all my hurts and frustrations down before God. I was angry, confused, hurt, and exhausted all at the same time. All I knew to do was to cry out to Him, while trying to stay true to the words I spoke to my wife, "Whatever is happening, we will walk in faith." That is when God intervened in my heart. What could have manifested itself as bitterness and resentment was calmed by the gentle words of my Lord to my heart: "Nathan, I am not doing this to you; I am doing this through you for someone else down the road."

These were not the words I wanted to hear, yet they were the words I needed. Though I didn't understand, I was able to get up with great confidence that God was going to do something amazing through our situation. I would only have to wait a few months for this to happen.

I was pastoring my first church in a rural setting. One Sunday afternoon, a couple I'd never met stopped by the church and needed to talk. They had just moved to the area and told me that they were driving by and something told them they should stop and speak to the pastor. Through God's sovereignty, I was able to lead them to faith in Jesus.

The story would be amazing if it stopped there. But as we began talking about what was going on in their lives, we learned they had just had a stillborn little girl. As we were ministering to them through this, we discovered that their little girl was not only buried in the same cemetery as our son, but in the next plot! The crazy thing is that the cemetery was thirty miles away. God redeemed our tragedy for His glory.

I tell you this lengthy story to show you that God is God, and we are not. We need to start believing that because He is God, He can do more than we could ever dream of. Many pastors and church leaders believe more in their own ability, networks, and resources than they do in God's power. This is the fleshly approach. We need to believe that God can do what God says He can do.

> **We need to start believing that because He is God, He can do more than we could ever dream of.**

I love the story in Ezekiel 37 where God places Ezekiel in the valley of dry bones. What ultimately becomes God's portrait of His ability to restore Israel has great implications for us as believers and for our faith. Of all the things that God shows Ezekiel in this vision, the main theme comes from the one question: "Can these bones live again?"

This question is what determines everything God will show him. It wasn't a question of God's ability; God knew He could do it. It wasn't a question of God's desire. If God wants to do it, He can. It was a question of Ezekiel's faith. Did he believe God could do it?

God is never as interested in our abilities or plans as He is in our faith in Him. Ezekiel had to trust that God was able to cause those bones to live again and that He was able to use Ezekiel in the process. Many pastors miss out on what God can do through them because they don't really believe that God can or wants to use them to help breathe new life into their churches and communities.

> **God is never as interested in our abilities or plans as He is in our faith in Him.**

One of the greatest assets that pastors can have is faith that God will do what God said He can do. What would our churches really look like if we operated in faith that God will show up? What if we prayed and obeyed expectantly? After all, what we believe will determine how we act. If we really believe God is big enough to save us from eternity in hell, shouldn't we believe that He can do things like restore marriages, bring in the needed funds for our churches, help churches grow through leading people to Christ? It is time we begin operating on faith and not on human ability.

Our strategy must leave room for God to say to us, "This is a huge vision; do you believe it can be done?" We must position ourselves and our churches to depend on God through faith. As someone once said, "Dream dreams so big that, unless God is in it, you're doomed for failure." This audacious faith can drive us to achieve greater things for the kingdom.

How does this play out in our churches and strategies? We must understand that God is not geographically inclined to move in any one place over another. He is not inclined to move more in one generation than another. God is God, and He is inclined to move where people are broken, dependent, desperate, and living in radical faith. So our churches must learn how to operate on God-sized faith to see God-sized things happen. This can be spurred on by answering two questions.

## IS OUR VISION LARGER THAN OUR ABILITY?

This question is of utmost importance to the future of your church. We often fall into the mindset that we must be enslaved to our abilities. Anytime we are operating within the parameters of our own abilities, we have no need for God. That's not what God is drawn to. We must get to the place in which we are dreaming things that only God can do. As pastors and leaders, we can rob our people of the blessing of seeing God do powerful things simply because our vision has no real faith aspect to it. People need to see the mighty hand of God move in their lives and church. But it requires a church taking a real faith journey to make it happen.

**WHAT ARE WE DOING NOW THAT REQUIRES REAL FAITH?**
This question helps us evaluate where we are with our current strategies and specifically denotes areas that require faith versus those that don't. In this evaluation, we should begin to be burdened toward total reliance on the Spirit of God moving in us. These are the revelations in us that allow us to equip our people to live faith-driven lives. Take the necessary steps today to ensure that your church family is doing things that require real faith in a real God.

No greater journey exists than the one that leads to a renewed faith in God's plan for you and your church. In moments of great faith, God breaks through and does the unimaginable. We have no good reason not to operate on great faith. God wants to do something great right where you are. He wants to breathe new life into your situation for His purposes and His agenda. As God placed Ezekiel in the valley of dry bones to be a change agent, God has placed you to usher your people into being a part of God's movement among you. I urge you today to begin pursuing the power of God like never before, and asking God to do things that would be otherwise impossible. For in this kind of faith, God is supremely glorified.

# CHAPTER 15

# Kingdom Growth:
## Transitioning Converts into Disciples

———⚓———

*Go therefore and make disciples of all the nations,
baptizing them in the name of the Father and the
Son and the Holy Spirit, teaching them to observe all
that I commanded you; and lo, I am with you always,
even to the end of the age.* – Matthew 28:19-20

Nothing quite tops the experience of having your first child. The excitement that begins in you the first time you realize you're going to be a parent is unparalleled. The baby showers, ultrasounds, and nursery decorating make memories that bring young couples closer together. The trip to the hospital to welcome the child into the world is the most fulfilling car ride one could ever ask for.

Once you get to the hospital, seconds feel like minutes and minutes like hours and hours like days. The anticipation of what it will be like to be Dad or Mom for the first time makes the waiting time both incredible and unbearable all at once. The moment you hear that child cry for the first time is the greatest imaginable sound. The first time you hold him or her, you find yourself wishing that time would just stand still. Then it happens. The thoughts start rushing through your mind, and you are faced with a question, "Now what?"

This is the same question many new believers ask. They may have "walked an aisle" or "prayed a prayer" to signify their desire to follow Christ. They have been baptized as a testimony of their newfound faith. But deep within their hearts, they may still be uncertain about what follows. It's all new to them, yet they may be surrounded by people who know the churchy lingo and who seem to know all the right answers. It's uncharted territory.

As pastors or leaders, we are to be passionate about winning people to faith in Christ. This should be a private practice as well as a corporate strategy. We should major on taking the gospel to those who are without Jesus. However, we cannot lead them to Christ and leave them at the altar. We cannot in good conscience celebrate their salvation in the baptistery, yet leave them there to face the future alone. We are just as accountable to teach and disciple them as we are to win them to Christ. Evangelism and discipleship are inextricably linked.

> **We are just as accountable to teach and disciple them as we are to win them to Christ.**

It's interesting that Jesus presented one of the most significant calls and challenges (some of the greatest words ever to grace mankind's ears) to His disciples right before He departed. Jesus gave the Great Commission to His disciples to instruct them to be thorough and complete in their ministry. This is vital in our church strategies today as well. When we dissect this challenge from Jesus, we see three great areas that inspire us.

## POSITION

Jesus had a message for His followers that would change the world. On top of that mountain, these disciples had no idea that Jesus would spell out their futures for them. They were still making sense of His death and His resurrection and intermittent presence over forty days. There in Galilee the words of Jesus did not only give them direction for the next few years, but they would reverberate across the centuries for our churches today.

Jesus knew that He was about to reveal the future of His church. But in His sovereignty, He wanted the disciples to remember that everything was about Him. He gave them their charge by first stating that He had been given all authority both in heaven and on earth. Why would Jesus begin with this? He wanted them to understand His position over them as Lord. Jesus made certain from the beginning that these men knew that He was the boss!

Also, Jesus wanted these men to know that there was nothing impossible when He was in the picture. He had all the authority and power to do whatever He wanted. Provided the disciples abided in Him, all things would be possible.

This is true for believers today. We must understand that Jesus can do anything He wishes. If we are wise, we will stay close to Him and depend on His power to help us in our ministries. We must fight the urge to believe that we have the authority and learn to trust in His authority. Jesus doesn't need us to accomplish His will; we need Him to help us as we seek to be a part of His will.

## PURPOSE

The amazing part of this passage is that the purpose of the church is unfolded in two verses. Jesus gives five main directives that pastors and leaders must grasp and embrace to fulfill the church's calling. These five directives will ultimately shape a church's strategy. They are:

**Go** – Jesus used strong language here. He commanded the disciples to go forward with the mission. We know the opposite of "stand still" is "go." We should be advancing the kingdom. Many pastors get caught up in the possible alternate Greek translations of the word "go," taking it to mean "as you are going." In the process of arguing over this nuance, we can lose the focus of what Jesus was saying. He was describing to His disciples a life of intentionality. By saying "go," Jesus was teaching that we must be active with the gospel when so many people are dying and in need of hope. We must go and go now!

**Make Disciples** – This statement is often downplayed in the local church. We reward numbers and baptisms. But how do you measure success in discipleship? Plaques and accolades don't mark the steady road of discipleship. In fact, it is the most unnoticed aspect of any church. This should not be the case. Jesus, at the beginning of the Great Commission, charged us to reproduce other disciples. As pastors and leaders, we must ensure the intentional discipleship of new believers. We can't lead them to Christ

> **We must take them by the hand and lead them to become more like Jesus.**

and baptize them merely to gain the praise of men. We must take them by the hand and lead them to become more like Jesus.

**All Nations** – I love this about the Great Commission. Jesus clearly communicated that our call is to world missions. It is to reach the nations for His glory. Have you ever thought that He could have left this phrase out? He didn't have to emphasize the nations in the Great Commission. But one who knows Jesus knows that His heart is for the nations. One of the greatest assets of a local church is its missions strategy. We lead people to be more like Jesus when we lead them to the nations.

**Baptizing** – This command in the Great Commission should come as no surprise. We know that in order to make disciples of the nations, we must lead them to faith in Christ. Jesus gave the command to baptize them. This is a great indicator of Jesus' desire to see people be eternally changed. Yes, we must tell them, we must disciple them, and we must help them walk in obedience through the testimony of baptism as well.

**Teaching** – A closing directive that Jesus gave to His disciples through the Great Commission was to be teachers of His commands. In order to reproduce Jesus in people, we must teach them about Jesus. Pastors and church leaders have the weighty responsibility to teach the Word faithfully to their people. This is not a command to teach that which will help your church grow. This is a command to stick to what Jesus has already spoken. We must reject soft and shallow teaching and embrace the deep truths of God's Word.

## PRESENCE

Jesus closed out the Great Commission by promising His disciples that they were not alone on this journey. He was walking with them as they followed His commands. The same is true with us and our churches. He is able, and He is stable. Jesus has not left you and your church on a deserted island. He knows exactly where you are and what you need. His promise to the disciples still stands today. He is with us and is here to help us.

So what does the Great Commission teach us to do in helping new converts become disciples of Christ? We are to be intentional with them, leading them to be obedient in baptism, discipling them to be more like Jesus, teaching them to obey His commands, and sending them out as missionaries among their circles of influence. Wow! What an awesome opportunity for the churches. We must engage the new believer and lead him or her on a journey of maturing faith. It's God's grand plan for the church.

You may be asking, "How does this play itself out in our churches?" As pastors and leaders, we must train our mature believers to be mentors for new converts. If we can pair the new convert with someone who has some life experience and years of walking in faith, they will learn not only by words but also by example. A one-on-one mentoring process will work wonders for someone who is new to the faith.

**When they experience serving in the church context, many times they fall in love with being used by God.**

Another great way to help transition new believers into those who are becoming more like Jesus is to assist them in finding places to serve. Experience is a great teacher. When they experience serving in the church context, many times they fall in love with being used by God. This will result in new believers getting excited about all that God wants to do in their lives.

We all need a team. None of us are lone rangers. Likewise, new believers need a small group of believers to connect and grow with. This will help them begin building important relationships. A person who builds relationships will likely want to engage in activities with whom they have built the relationship. This will place them around other believers more and will result in a maturing of their faith. Even today, I have a small group of men that I am in constant contact with. We are walking through similar seasons of life and are always encouraging one another to look more like Jesus! It is crucial for new believers to have a support group to grow and be challenged in their walk with the Lord.

Simply stated, we can't merely reach them; we must also teach them for a lifetime. Our job is not over after someone responds to the invitation. In fact, our job has just begun at that point. It is exciting to see someone come to faith in Christ. Yet it is even more exciting to watch them grow and lead others to Christ themselves. That is the Great Commission in action.

# CHAPTER 16

# Conclusion:
## The Paradigm Shift

———————— ⚓ ————————

This book was written to challenge the idea of church growth over kingdom growth. Somewhere along the way, we became enamored with the idea of ministerial success and abandoned evangelism and the larger Great Commission mandate of disciple-making. This is not the heart of our Lord for His church. We must return to a place where evangelism and the gospel drive everything we do.

Let me be clear: Numerical growth is a good thing for a Christ-centered, gospel-proclaiming church. The desire for more people is not bad. In fact, I'd be wary of any pastor who has no vision or ambition to see his flock increase. Yet if all we are doing is swapping sheep or drawing spiritual thrill seekers for the sake of numbers or reputation, then the kingdom is not really being advanced. We must change the paradigm. Evangelism must be our strategy for biblical growth. Pastors and church leaders, please ponder these two final challenges that I believe will influence your church and further the kingdom:

## MAKE EVANGELISM YOUR PRIMARY PURPOSE

I challenge you to make evangelism your primary purpose. It is the only thing that can have a substantial and eternal impact upon your community. Methods and models are penned by the hands of men. Transformed lives are penned by the hand of God. This is what evangelism does. I understand that a church's structure is often complex, and there are many different ministries that need to function through your church. Nonetheless, I plead with you to make sure everything that you do at your church has evangelism at its heart. Your church can experience its greatest growth if you will intentionally incorporate evangelism as its primary purpose and into the DNA of every ministry.

## EXPECT GOD TO DO SOMETHING GREAT

I also challenge you to expect God to show up in your church. We are living in the greatest days ever to be a Christian. We have more tools available to share Christ than ever before. But to seize the moment, we must believe that God will use us to accomplish great things for the kingdom.

We must take risks. We must be adventurous with the gospel. We must position ourselves and our churches to exercise great faith in a great God! Our strategies are needed, but even more than that, our dependence on God and guidance from Him are essential to accomplish what He would have for us. This is when I believe we will see a movement of God greater than the world has ever known.

God wants to do great things in and through you. Stand firm, stay rooted in the Word of God, and walk humbly before our King. With that, I believe that the greatest days for you and your church are yet to come!

# Evangelism Models in the Modern Church

Many different kinds of evangelism models or strategies exist in churches today. Some have been around for many years while others are new. In all types of evangelism, the goal is the same: to win people to Christ through sharing the gospel. As the reader will see, the gospel can be shared in many different ways through local church ministry. This list is not exhaustive but will give a general understanding of the different models we see today.

## MODEL #1: DOOR-TO-DOOR

Door-to-door evangelism has been around since the New Testament church. In fact, this model has for many years been a preferred method of evangelism in the local church. Many churches have called this "visitation night," a time in which people go out in teams door to door to share their faith or to share about their church.

Over the years, various evangelism curricula such as F.A.I.T.H. and Evangelism Explosion have been created with door-to-door evangelism in mind. These modes of sharing the gospel have created a cookie-cutter approach to door-to-door evangelism. They seem to work well and are better than no strategy at all. As long as a church is being prayerful and intentional about going out and sharing the gospel, any method will work. In fact, the only thing that doesn't work is doing nothing at all!

This model of evangelism has both fans and critics. Most will say it is still a model that can succeed, while a few believe it is a thing of the past. The context of the area your church is in needs to be taken into account. Rural areas may be much more difficult with this approach than perhaps a highly populated city in which houses are close together. Nevertheless, many churches continue to use it weekly.

Door-to-door evangelism has produced many converts to Christ. It has also served as a launching pad for many new church plants. It is a method that has stood the test of time but must ultimately be examined in each church's context in order to determine its usefulness.

## MODEL #2: EVENT

One of the more commonly used models of evangelism is event-based evangelism. Evangelistic events aim to draw as many people as possible, and they are often successful in terms of seeing people won to Christ. Event evangelism is popular in churches today because it often yields instantaneous results. This gets a pastor and a church excited and can usher a church into a season of great growth and momentum.

These events take shape as block parties, revivals, sports-related gatherings, outdoor concerts, and other activities. But event evangelism can be costly, and like any such venture, winning mass numbers to Christ is never guaranteed. Therefore, churches must understand their cultural surroundings in deciding which types of events are best for them.

## MODEL #3: RELATIONSHIP

Relationship evangelism tends to be a popular approach in today's churches. People also have a tendency to call this model "friendship evangelism." This approach can be traced back to the life of Jesus as He sought to know people when He shared with them. A great example in the Bible is the woman at the well (John 4:7-42). This woman was minding her own business collecting water when Jesus engaged her in conversation. He led the conversation in a way that pointed her to faith, yet it was very personal in nature.

Relationship evangelism has many benefits and some obstacles. However, it seems to be the most natural form of evangelism to most people. Despite whether one believes that he or she has the gift of evangelism or not, engaging people with the gospel in the natural rhythms of life through friendships and relationships is doable for everyone.

## MODEL #4: PRACTICAL MINISTRY

Practical ministry evangelism is a model utilizing various types of evangelism as people's immediate needs are met. Examples of this type would be food pantries, clothes closets, helping people with prescriptions, and general benevolence. These types of opportunities come at a time in which people are in need. Often, showing kindness earns credibility in order to speak into a person's life. This type of evangelism is one that people and churches can use daily. It gives churches an opportunity to be like the church in Acts 4:34, which says, For there was not a needy person among them. This could once again be the reputation of the church if this evangelism model was taken seriously.

**MODEL #5: MARKETING**

The idea of marketing evangelism seems to have increased in the last two decades. Many churches have used modern marketing tools to share the gospel. These types of tools fall into the categories of billboards, mass mailers, clothing, and any other form of marketing that shares the gospel. American society has become dependent upon marketing in order to gain information.

Many churches have bought into this new craze. They have taken full advantage of the opportunities that marketing affords and have utilized it for evangelism. While there are many great things about using marketing as an evangelism outlet, dangers exist as well. A church must decide where marketing fits in its budget and strategy. A marketing church will often find itself needing to be increasingly innovative. This can be a fun venture, or it can become burdensome over time.

**MODEL #6: SERVANT**

Servant evangelism is one of the models that has been around since the Bible was written. And it seems as if this model of evangelism is making a comeback in the church. Central to servant evangelism is sharing the love of Christ not only in word but also in deed. This model is one through which many people who do not feel bold enough to share their faith in words can still help bring people to Christ.

Servant evangelism is a method that is backed up by the words of Jesus when He said, the Son of Man did not come to be served, but to serve (Matthew 20:28). At the core of this mindset is the belief that a believer can be like Jesus in serving while allowing people to take notice of the gospel being lived out. This model is often found in churches that have a heart to reach those who are struggling economically.

Ultimately, words must accompany deeds for the gospel message to take root in one's heart. But what cannot be debated is the fact that Christ was a servant. Therefore, the life of Christ obligates believers to live out their faith in love and service. A church must determine if that can be done in the form of intentional servant evangelism.

## MODEL #7: SOCIALLY DRIVEN PROGRAMS

Churches in the western world are filled with programs. The mindset has been that programs reach people or at least keep them busy in the Lord's work. But many churches never strategically look at their programs as evangelistic tools. There are many whose sole purpose can be evangelism. Three specific types of socially driven programs exist. First, age-specific programs include AWANA, Team Kids, handbells, and senior adult trips. All of these programs are designed for a targeted age and are therefore somewhat exclusive.

A second type that can be used evangelistically is the program that is specific to circumstances or stages. Such programs include divorce care, singles ministry, grief classes, and marriage-enrichment programs. These programs target a situation that someone is going through and can be a great tool to share the gospel in a time of need or tragedy in someone's life.

A third category includes special-interest programs such as a civic club, a businessmen's Bible study, or a weight-loss program. These programs target certain subsets of people and often draw people through the doors who have never expressed interest in church. Program-driven evangelism is not the end, but it is a means to the end.

Evangelism is not a program but can be integrated into programs in order to share the gospel. Churches must consider the ultimate goal of their programs. Where the goal is not being met, churches can add or take programs away.

## MODEL #8: MISSIONS EVANGELISM

Missions and evangelism go hand in hand. But missions can be the engine that drives evangelism. A model that is often used in churches but not often recognized as an intentional evangelism model is missions evangelism. This is the strategy wherein churches get people involved in mission opportunities, both local and international. These mission projects or trips can profoundly impact a person and a church. In particular, mission trips can lead to a more evangelistic church at home. Mission projects and trips are primarily for evangelism beyond the community, but they also increase fervor at the local church level.

Churches with a missions model of evangelism tend to be larger in size. This is usually because they will have more people to send. But small churches can utilize this model as well. It can give them the boost they need in order to further the kingdom's cause throughout their body. Every church can implement a missions strategy that will affect the church and help reach the lost people of the world.

## MODEL #9: STREET

Street evangelism is a model that has been successful in certain areas. In fact, in highly populated areas this can be a real winning strategy. In most cases, this type of evangelism is done in a way that draws people in to hear the gospel. However, this model takes boldness. Churches will often have an evangelism team that will go out to a street corner or a park and begin street preaching.

Throughout the years, many have come into a relationship with Christ through street preaching or evangelism. In fact, Kirk Cameron and Ray Comfort have become nationally known for their unique type of street evangelism through their ministry called The Way of the Master. This type of evangelism strategy is geared toward meeting people where they are. People are engaged with the gospel within their comfort zone rather than within the walls of a church.

Street evangelism over the years has had a great potential to draw people in who would ordinarily not be able to attend a church or religious gathering. Another strong benefit to this approach is that people who were not expecting to be engaged with the gospel have not had the time to prepare their minds to reject the gospel message.

## MODEL #10: MEDIA

Media evangelism is a relatively new approach to sharing the gospel which many churches are taking advantage of. In fact, in today's society this has become a relatively easy and effective way of presenting the life-changing message of Christ. This form of evangelism is done in many different ways, four of which are briefly examined below.

## MODEL #10.1: SOCIAL WEBSITES

The opportunity to share the gospel with a mass number of people is available at the fingertips of many today on social websites. Popular websites like Facebook, Myspace, and Twitter give the church an open market to share the gospel without fear of reprimand. This is a great avenue in which people can dialogue and share their faith in a non-threatening way.

## MODEL #10.2: TELEVISION AND MOVIES

Another source of media evangelism comes from television and movies. For many years there has been a significant presence of televangelists and Christian television networks. While this is a form that often draws criticism, it has been very effective. Along with television, a new movement has used movies as an evangelistic tool. In the past few years, many Christian movies such as Courageous, Fireproof, and Facing the Giants have shared the gospel in a clear manner. Movies can be a great tool because of their ability to stir the emotions of the heart.

## MODEL #10.3: RADIO

Radio evangelism is still used around the world today. Churches often have their services live on the radio, or they can create a talk-show program. Whatever means are used on the radio can still be counted as effective. Radio may eventually become less effective, but for now it is still a valuable method that is being used.

## MODEL #10.4: MEDIA CAMPAIGN

A final method that is being used with some success is a media campaign. A great example of this is IAmSecond.com.[21] This website is a campaign that draws people by featuring celebrities, such as Albert Pujols and Josh Turner, as well as ordinary people who have come to faith. They tell their stories, such as Brian Welch who formerly was a part of the band Korn. He tells about his deep drug abuse and then shares the gospel. Other forms of this include video-driven evangelism, such as the Nooma video series from Mars Hill Church in Grand Rapids, Michigan. This type of approach is quickly gaining ground.

## MODEL #11: CRISIS

Crisis evangelism has a love/hate relationship with the church. Churches love the opportunity to share Christ with people, but they hate that the opportunity has to come at the expense of someone going through a crisis. But crises often prove to be a small window during which people are the most open to the gospel.

This type of evangelism is only used periodically as a circumstance would allow it to be used. This is not necessarily a method that a church builds into its evangelism strategy. It is, however, a method that the church needs to be ready to use when the opportunity presents itself. Crisis evangelism must be sensitive to the situation yet stand ready to take full advantage to share the gospel. An example of this type of evangelism opportunity occurs after catastrophes like 9/11 or Hurricane Katrina. Churches must seize the moment to share the message of hope in crisis.

Many churches today do not engage in this type of evangelism simply because they are so inwardly focused that they never see the need. They never grasp the crisis because they never become aware of the difficulties the people around them are experiencing. This form of evangelism may be the only opportunity people have to hear the answer they are searching for, and churches need to stand ready to provide that answer.

**MODEL #12: SERVANT/EVENT**
This model of evangelism is one of the most effective of all methods. This model is the compilation of servant and event-driven methods, and it recognizes that people have the opportunity to serve others while at the same time being able to share the gospel with the masses. This method creates an environment within the church in which everyone can be a part of the Great Commission.

# Ideas for Evangelism in Your Church

## Evangelism Events and Ideas

E vangelism can and should be an exciting part of our lives and the life of our churches. These types of events and ideas will not only reach the lost and the unchurched, but they will encourage the congregation and help open the church's eyes to the great needs around the community. The number of events that can be done is unlimited. However, here are fifteen particular events that seem to work well and produce results for the kingdom of God.

**BLOCK PARTIES**

Block parties have been around for many years. They can be one of the most effective tools a church can use to get its foot in the door of many communities around it. This particular strategy worked very well in the last church I pastored. We made it a priority to identify the communities that were unreached and had great needs. The church built a process in which it could move into a community and set up for a block party within twenty minutes. The block parties are publicized about a week ahead of the party.

When going into a neighborhood, our church identified a place in which a Bible study could be started with a church in the immediate area with which they could partner. This allows the partnering church to reap the benefits of any new believers who would come as a result of the block party.

A church that goes into a community and hosts a block party needs to offer things that appeal to the residents of that neighborhood or community. These things can be anything from inflatable toys and waterslides to low-budget foods such as hot dogs that will fit easily into any church's budget. If people know that they will be fed and that their families will have fun and be safe, they will be much more likely to come and take part in the event.

Block parties are an excellent springboard to engage unbelievers and unchurched people. They provide the local congregation an opportunity to meet people where they are and serve them with the love of Christ. A church that hosts block parties will want to register the attendees to ensure quick and well-organized follow-up. This is a great way to personally connect on the people's territory.

## FALL FESTIVALS

Fall festivals are another great way for churches to reach out to their community with a big event. Fall festivals are typically hosted around Halloween in order to capitalize on the kids' desire to participate in trick-or-treating. This type of event takes an enormous number of volunteers but can reap some great results.

Fall festivals can be done inside or outside. Of course, any time an event is planned for outside, it runs the risk of bad weather. Churches that choose to use this form of servant/event evangelism must always have a backup plan in place, in case of unpredictable weather.

An event like this succeeds if the leader enlists Sunday school classes or Life Groups to host booths and games in which the children can play. A fall festival works well on Halloween because it offers families a fun, safe alternative to neighborhood trick-or-treating. If a family knows they can come to a safe place where their children can play games and receive candy, they will be more likely to come.

This type of event benefits the church in two ways. First, it provides unity for the church as people meet to prepare for the event. Second, this event provides opportunities to educate the community about the opportunities for children's ministry provided by the church.

Another great benefit of hosting a fall festival is the opportunity to share the gospel to what may be the largest gathering of people the church will have all year. The church should take advantage of that opportunity at some point during the evening. Due to the high level of impact this event can have, it is one that churches should consider implementing into their evangelistic strategy.

**EASTER EGG HUNT**
Easter is another wonderful opportunity to reach unchurched families with young children. This provides a chance for churches to not only have a large crowd in service on Easter

Sunday but also to go the extra mile to reach out to the children. When done well, this event can produce many opportunities with somewhat minimal effort. This event can be done in many ways, and churches must allow their budgets to dictate the particulars. But it can be as simple as providing eggs for kids to hunt while attempting to connect with their parents. This type of event also gives another opportunity for churches to share the gospel at a time of the year when people are open to hearing the message.

One of the keys to making this event a success is to hold the event in a safe place. Parents notice when a church goes the extra mile to strive for safety for their children. An Easter egg hunt also provides a church the opportunity to expose the parents of the children involved to all the opportunities the church has for their family.

## EASTER DRAMA

Hosting an Easter drama is another way to reap results for the kingdom of God at a special time of the year. This event provides churches with the opportunity to share the gospel message with the unchurched in a more entertaining way. A drama takes a lot of participation by church members, but it will also create a unifying spirit during the holiday season.

Easter dramas can relate to people in a way that worship services often cannot. Churches that put the gospel into a drama will draw people who are passionate about the arts. These people often would not be interested in a typical church service but may be inclined to come to a dramatic production.

There are three crucial aspects to seeing great results in an Easter drama. First, a church must make sure that Jesus is the ultimate subject of the drama. People need to hear the gospel and in many cases see it played out before their eyes. The death, burial, and resurrection of Jesus must be at the forefront of this effort.

Second, churches need to have a sufficient number of volunteers greeting people and helping them find seats. People will feel welcomed if they are personally greeted and assisted upon their arrival.

A third crucial aspect is to have something special for kids to do during the drama. Many times dramas contain violent depictions of the crucifixion, so it is a good idea to provide children with an alternative activity that shares the gospel in a less violent manner. This can be a significant element in a parent's decision to come to the event.

A church needs to capitalize on Easter dramas by publicizing well before the event. Churches must make it a priority to get the word out. It is a great idea to get as many media outlets as possible to do stories on the drama in order to help publicize it. In this way, Easter dramas can be effective.

## COMMUNITY CAR WASHES AND CLINICS

Other events in which churches can experience great results are community car washes and clinics. These events provide the community with a chance to see churched people serving on the weekends. A great time to host this type of event is during late spring through early fall. A community car wash or clinic will help people to get one-on-one time with guests. It also provides members the opportunity to connect with people in an environment in which they might be receptive.

One of the greatest aspects of a community car wash or clinic is that it is provided at no cost. This opens the door to the idea that the church is simply there to serve out of love, which is something that the unchurched do not see or experience often. This can be a great pathway for the gospel to be shared to each of the people present.

Churches can also do car care clinics for single mothers and widows. This can involve, but is not limited to, oil changes, air filter replacement, tire rotation, and other basic auto services. Churches can identify single mothers and widows, which in turn will facilitate follow-up for future ministry. When a church serves in this capacity, unchurched people begin to see that it is not a group of exclusive people sitting behind the walls of a church building. This kind of event can be costly to a church but will allow the church to connect with people in difficult situations and will provide great ministry opportunities for the future.

## GAS BUY-DOWN

One way to implement an evangelism strategy in the midst of a difficult economic time is for a church to sponsor a gas buy-down day at a local gas station. Churches can pay a gas station in advance to offer gas at a reduced rate for the community to purchase. This type of event will generate a busy day of ministry and opportunity.

The strategy for this event is that for a two- or three-hour period, a church offers people gas at a discounted rate. People pull up to the pump, one church member pumps their gas, and another washes the windshield. At the same time, another person gives the customer a bottle of water and briefly shares the gospel with them.

This event allows people to see the church out in the community, doing something for the people. This has the potential to generate a lot of attention that can be beneficial to the church. However, gas buy-downs come with a hefty price tag. A church must understand that the costly event will provide the chance to have some individual time with the customers. In addition, it also gives the church a chance to partner with a local business and let the community know that it cares about the community. When the heart of a church is burdened to help the community in a time of need, they have the potential of seeing great results.

## MARRIAGE CONFERENCE

Another event that is timely for today is a free marriage conference. This event will address a specific need that could lead to a fruitful harvest for churches. Marriages are falling apart in all regions of the United States. A marriage conference provides an opportunity for churches to reach couples that are struggling or who are on the brink of divorce.

In addition, it will give churches a captive audience to explain the fact that only God can help a marriage. People are hurting and looking for help, and the church can share the hope that is only found by inviting God into the marriage. A conference such as this will not produce as many attendees as other events, but it will provide attendees that are open to the gospel because of their circumstances.

A marriage conference can also lead to opportunities for the church to reach out to its community. People who come to this type of event will connect in a way that would not ordinarily happen. A conference can be costly, but the joy of seeing God work in marriages that society would have forgotten outweighs the cost of the event.

## SPORTSMAN'S EXPO

Another great opportunity for churches is a sportsman's expo. Many men and possibly some ladies will participate. A sportsman's expo can be specifically geared toward one sport, or it can be general in nature. It can be as simple or elaborate as a church wants to make it. Some costs will be associated with it, but this occasion could bridge the gap between churches and local businesses. If a church contacts businesses and invites them to be sponsors, the cost of the event can be reduced. A sportsman's expo will also bring these businesses great exposure to people of the community.

## FOURTH OF JULY

A Fourth of July extravaganza is another great way to reach the people of a community. Many people love the idea of watching fireworks but cannot afford them. This is where a church can step in and provide a family-friendly atmosphere in which to celebrate the nation's independence together, but it also provides a chance for a pastor or leader to share how the gospel leads us to spiritual freedom.

A Fourth of July event will require two things. First, it needs to be publicized well in advance. Families will to go to what they deem to be the most attractive fireworks show. Therefore, a church must make sure that it is well equipped for a large fireworks show. A family will sit through a thorough gospel presentation if they know that they will be blessed by the light show. A second aspect that needs to be implemented into this event is food. Churches must weigh charging for the food versus providing it for free.

A Fourth of July event will allow a church to touch a large number of people with little effort. However, a church needs to be well prepared to register all the families at the event so that it follows up with them soon after the event. This type of event will show unchurched families that the church cares for them and is there to minister to them.

## BACK-TO-SCHOOL BASH

A back-to-school bash can produce many opportunities for churches. This is especially true if the church gives away free school supplies to children. Such an event will resemble a block party with inflatable toys and food. However, it also gives churches the opportunity to share the gospel with a large group of people.

The people who will receive free school supplies will likely be in need of them. This gives the church a chance to tell these people how much it cares for them. This mindset will open doors for the church to connect with people and allow the church to help them in their needs.

A back-to-school bash needs solely to focus on the children and youth of a community. The bash should be a high-energy day in which families come and have a great time. The best time to do this is within two weeks prior to the school year beginning. This will help to alleviate stress in parents who are wondering how they are going to get school supplies for their children.

## CHRISTMAS TREE GIVEAWAY

Christmas time each year provides wonderful opportunities for churches to engage people with the gospel of Jesus. People usually have real needs during this time of year, which means that people are more open to hear about the hope that is found in Christ. Churches that want to utilize this holiday can do so by hosting an event. One of the best events to hold is a Christmas tree giveaway. Churches can partner with local Christmas tree farms to negotiate a lower price for the less desirable trees. This will fit into the church's budget and will still provide an opportunity for churches to engage the people of the community.

One of the main benefits of this type of event is that it makes the children of families that receive trees very happy. Typically, these children will not have a tree for Christmas, but churches can give this gift while also giving the gift of Jesus. This event will touch the hearts of young families who may be going through a difficult time and provide ministry opportunities for the church.

## CHRISTMAS STORE

A Christmas store will allow a church to reach those who have fallen on hard times by meeting an immediate need. Churches should contact local schools and ask for a list of children who will not have Christmas gifts unless they receive assistance. Members can begin buying gifts in October and bring them to the church.

The leader of this event should contact each family and ask about their situation. This will be the first step in opening the door of communication with these families. Once a date is set the families should be contacted and told when and where to arrive to get the gifts for their children.

When the family arrives, there needs to be a process they go through to choose their gifts. The church should have a host for each family who will walk them through the process. After the family selects all the gifts, the host should lead them to the gift-wrapping table. This is where the opportunity to share the gospel begins.

Families have the opportunity to have refreshments and sit at a table with their host. It is here that the host will share the gospel and seek out other needs that the family may have. This kind of event allows many people in the church to be involved in serving while also making sure that the gospel is shared with every parent who comes through the doors.

## FRIDAY NIGHT FOOTBALL TAILGATING

A great thing for churches to do in the fall is a football tailgating party. A church can do this for one game or for every game. A church can give out free food and T-shirts, which will encourage the people to come. This is relatively inexpensive and has the potential to touch many people on a Friday night.

A football party works well in small towns. Friday night football is a big deal in many places across the country, and churches can take advantage of this by being a real presence in the community on these nights. It also helps the community see that the church supports the local schools and the children who attend them. While this type of event will certainly be contextual, it often brings with it an excitement that other events can lack.

## CRUSADE

One of the oldest and most effective servant events that churches host are crusades. The goal of a crusade is to get as many people as possible to come to a certain place. Crusades have been very successful for many years and have seen millions of people come to faith in Christ. One of the crucial elements for a crusade is a full-time evangelist, who will be gifted in sharing the gospel and drawing in the net during the invitation time. Many churches have forgotten this method or have deemed it irrelevant for today's society. However, a church that does this with excellence will see excellent results.

The key to this event is being prepared and having enough publicity and volunteers. A crusade will need to be advertised all over the community. Each night can be a different emphasis in order to engage all different age groups. When done well, these special emphases draw in hundreds of people each night to hear the gospel.

## THANKSGIVING MEAL

A Thanksgiving meal for the community also holds great potential. This event will let the people of the community know that the church cares for them at a special time of the year and will give exposure to the church. A Thanksgiving meal does not need an enormous number of volunteers if the church has the meals catered. In this way, it provides the members an opportunity to focus on loving the people of the community relationally.

The major roadblock for this event is space limitations. When a church provides a free meal to the community, there is no way of estimating the turnout. This can make preparation a problem. Therefore, the church should secure a large-enough space to host at least three times its total church attendance.

A Thanksgiving meal allows the pastor to share the gospel with a large number of people who will be open to hearing it as a result of the church's generosity to them. This is also a great opportunity to have scheduled testimonies from people showing how God has radically changed their lives through various events.

If a church cannot find space or funds for a full meal, there is an alternative. Churches can give away Thanksgiving dinners to families who are in need. This happens when members identify needy families and show up at their house with a full Thanksgiving dinner.

# About the Author

D r. Nathan Lorick is the Director of Evangelism for the Southern Baptists of Texas Convention. He works directly with churches across Texas to engage their communities with the gospel. His desire is to glorify God and see the church come alive through intentional evangelism and missions, making a positive difference in this generation. He currently serves as a trustee for the International Mission Board of the Southern Baptist Convention. He is a graduate of East Texas Baptist University and Liberty Baptist Theological Seminary where he earned both a Masters of Divinity and Doctor of Ministry degree. He also holds an Honorary Doctor of Divinity from Louisiana Baptist University. He and his wife Jenna live in Texas with their 4 children.

Nathan has been a guest on media outlets such as "Fox and Friends", "Glen Beck Radio", "American Family Radio", "Tony Perkins Live" and many others for taking a stand for religious freedom. His passion to see culture transformed by the power of the gospel sets him apart in his generation. He is a sought out speaker who unashamedly unveils the truths of Scripture concerning today's most pressing issues. When not travelling Nathan enjoys spending time with his family, hunting, reading and running.

**Connect with Nathan**

Website: www.NathanLorick.com

Twitter: @NathanLorick

Facebook: www.facebook.com/nathan.lorick

Book Speaking Engagements: nathan@nathanlorick.com

# Endnotes

1   Ed Stetzer and Warren Bird, *Vital Churches: Helping Church Planters Become Movement Makers* (San Francisco, CA: Jossey-Bass-Wiley, 2010).

2   Thom S. Rainer, *Breakout Churches: Discover How to Make the Leap* (Grand Rapids, MI: Zondervan, 2005).

3   David Platt, *Follow Me: A Call to Die. A Call to Live* (Carol Stream, IL: Tyndale House Publishers, 2013), (foreword) 17.

4   Ed Stetzer, *Planting Missional Churches* (Nashville, TN: Broadman and Holman Publishers, 2006), 317.

5   Rick Warren, *The Purpose Driven Church: Every Church is Big in God's Eyes* (Grand Rapids, MI: Zondervan, 1995), 66.

6   Kenneth O. Gangel, *Team Leadership in Christian Ministry: Using Multiple Gifts to Build a Unified Vision* (Chicago, IL: Moody Bible Institute of Chicago, 1997), 290.

7   Leith Anderson, "Volunteer Recruitment," in *Leadership Handbook of Management and Administration,* ed. James D. Berkley (Grand Rapids, MI: Baker Books, 2007), 312.

8   Ahn Che, *Spirit-Led Evangelism: Reaching the Lost through Love and Power* (Grand Rapids, MI: Chosen Books, 2006).

9   Roger N. McNamara and Ken Davis, *The Y-B-H Handbook of Church Planting (Yes, But How?)* (Xulon Press, 2005), 416.

10  Darrell W. Robinson, *Total Church Life: How to Be a First Century Church* (Nashville, TN: Broadman and Holman Publishers, 1997).

11  David Bracken and Carol W. Timmreck and Allan H. Church, eds., *The Handbook of Multisource Feedback* (San Francisco, CA: Jossey-Bass, Inc., 2001), 359.

12  Darrel Vaughan, *Do You Know How to Pray as You Should?* (Mustang, OK: Tate Publishing & Enterprises, LLC, 2009), 71.

13  Lon Allison and Mark Anderson, *Going Public With the Gospel: Reviving Evangelistic Proclamation* (Downers Grove, IL: InterVarsity Press, 2003), 160.

14  Nelson Searcy and Jennifer Henson, *Fusion: Turning First-Time Guests into Fully-Engaged Members of Your Church* (Ventura, CA: Regal Publishers, 2007), 142.

15  Aubrey Malphurs, *Advanced Strategic Planning: A New Model for Church and Ministry Leaders* (Grand Rapids, MI: Baker Books, 2005), 161.

16  Ryan J. Doeller, *Marketing God to Teens* (Bloomington, IN: Xlibris Corporation, 2010), 44.

17  North American Mission Board, www.namb.net.

18  Timothy L. Webster, *Christ-Centered Pastors: Four Essentials Pastors Must Do To Focus On Christ, Not Man* (Bloomington, IN: CrossBooks, 2010), 290.

19  Patrick Morley, *Pastoring Men: What Works, What Doesn't, and Why It Matters Now More Than Ever* (Chicago, IL: Moody Publishers, 2009), 104.

20  Brian J. Dodd, *Empowered Church Leadership: Ministry in the Spirit According to Paul* (Downers Grove, IL: InterVarsity Press, 2003), 175.

21  www.iamsecond.com

# Bibliography

Ahn, Che. *Spirit-Led Evangelism: Reaching the Lost through Love and Power.* Grand Rapids: Chosen Books, 2006.

Allison, Lon, and Mark Anderson. *Going Public with the Gospel: Reviving Evangelistic Proclamation.* Downers Grove: InterVarsity Press, 2003.

Anderson, Leith. "Volunteer Recruitment." In *Leadership Handbook of Management and Administration,* edited by James D. Berkley. Grand Rapids: Baker Books, 2007.

Bracken, David W., Carol W. Timmreck, and Allan H. Church, eds., *The Handbook of Multisource Feedback.* San Francisco: Jossey-Bass Inc., 2001.

Dodd, Brian J. *Empowered Church Leadership: Ministry in the Spirit According to Paul.* Downers Grove: InterVarsity Press, 2003.

Doeller, Ryan J. *Marketing God to Teens.* Bloomington: Xlibris Corporation, 2010.

Gangel, Kenneth O. *Team Leadership in Christian Ministry: Using Multiple Gifts to Build a Unified Vision.* Chicago: Moody Bible Institute, 1997.

Malphurs, Aubrey. *Advanced Strategic Planning: A New Model for Church and Ministry Leaders.* Grand Rapids: Baker Books, 2005.

McNamara, Roger N. and Ken Davis. *The Y-B-H Handbook of Church Planting (Yes, But How?).* Xulon Press, 2005.

Morley, Patrick. *Pastoring Men: What Works, What Doesn't, and Why It Matters Now More Than Ever.* Chicago: Moody Publishers, 2009.

North American Mission Board. www.namb.net.

Platt, David. *Follow Me: A Call to Die. A Call to Live.* Carol Stream: Tyndale, 2013.

Rainer, Thom S. *Breakout Churches: Discover How to Make the Leap.* Grand Rapids: Zondervan, 2005.

Robinson, Darrel W. *Total Church: How to Be a First Century Church.* Nashville: Broadman and Holman Publishers, 1997.

Searcy, Nelson and Jennifer Henson. *Fusion: Turning First-Time Guests into Fully-Engaged Members of Your Church.* Ventura: Regal, 2007.

Stetzer, Ed. *Planting Missional Churches.* Nashville: Broadman and Holman Publishers, 2006.

Stetzer, Ed and Warren Bird. *Viral Churches: Helping Church Planters Become Movement Makers.* San Francisco: Jossey-Bass: A Wiley Imprint, 2010.

Vaughan, Darrel. *Do You Know How to Pray As You Should?* Mustang: Tate Publishing & Enterprises, LLC, 2009.

Warren, Rick. *The Purpose Driven Church: Every Church is Big in God's Eyes.* Grand Rapids: Zondervan, 1995.

Webster, Timothy L. *Christ-Centered Pastors: Four Essentials Pastors Must Do to Focus on Christ, Not Man.* Bloomington: CrossBooks, 2010.

www.iamsecond.com

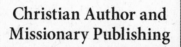